DINOSAUR COLOR BOOK
Super Fun Edition

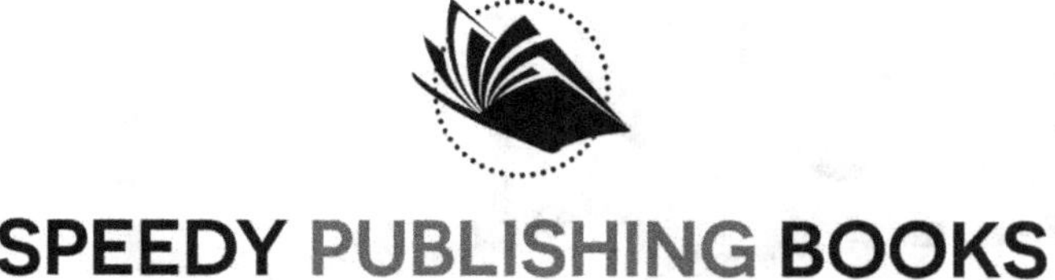

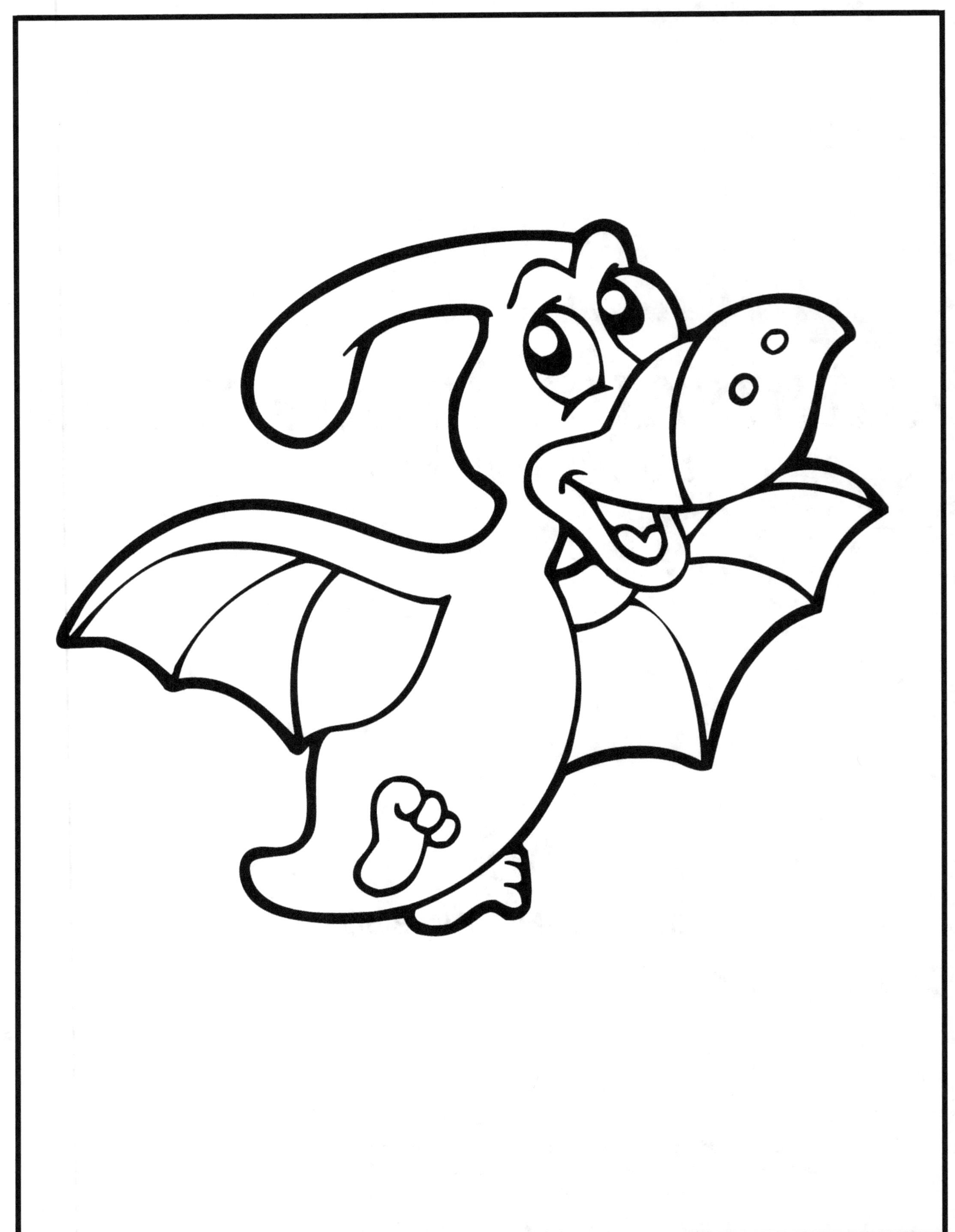

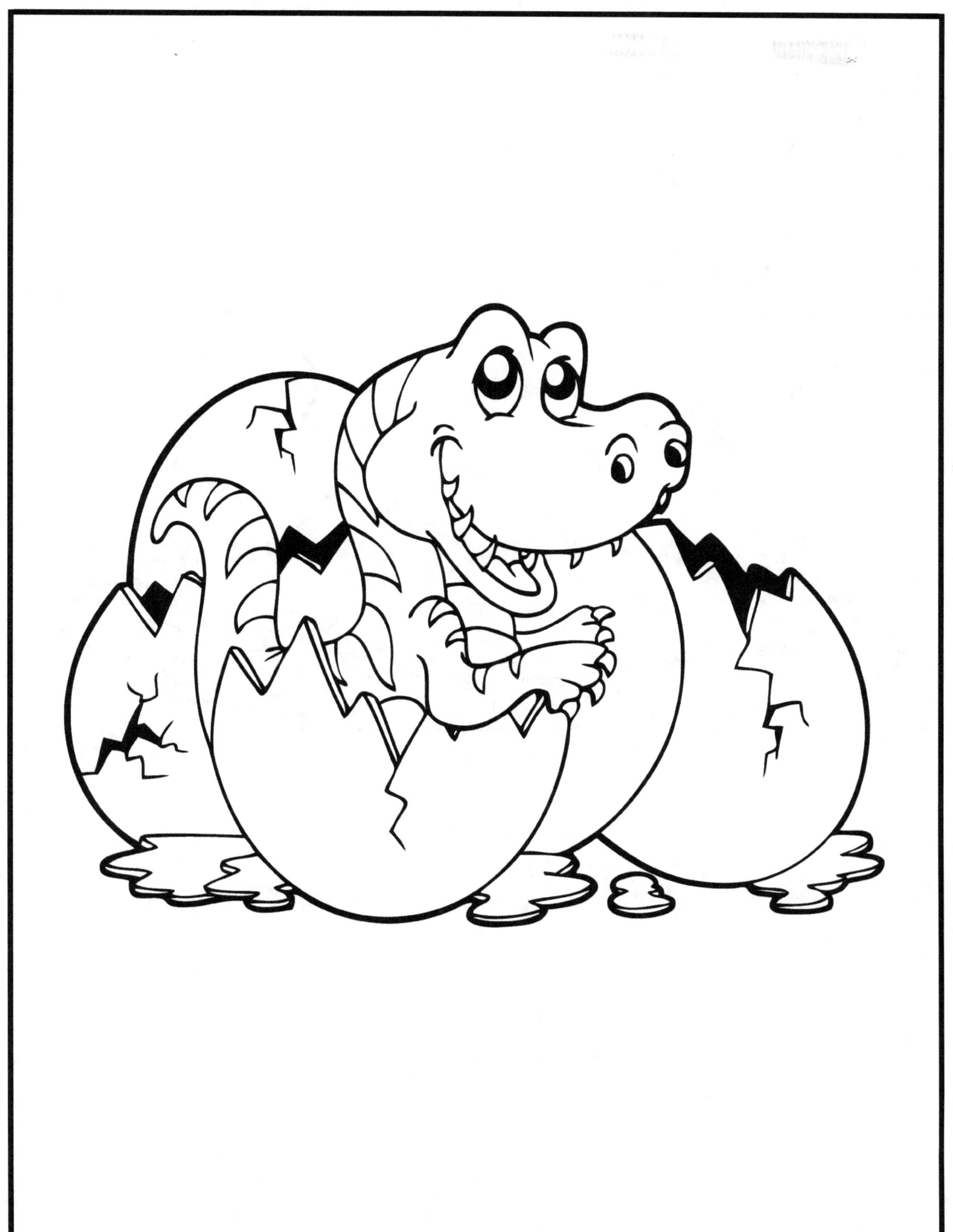

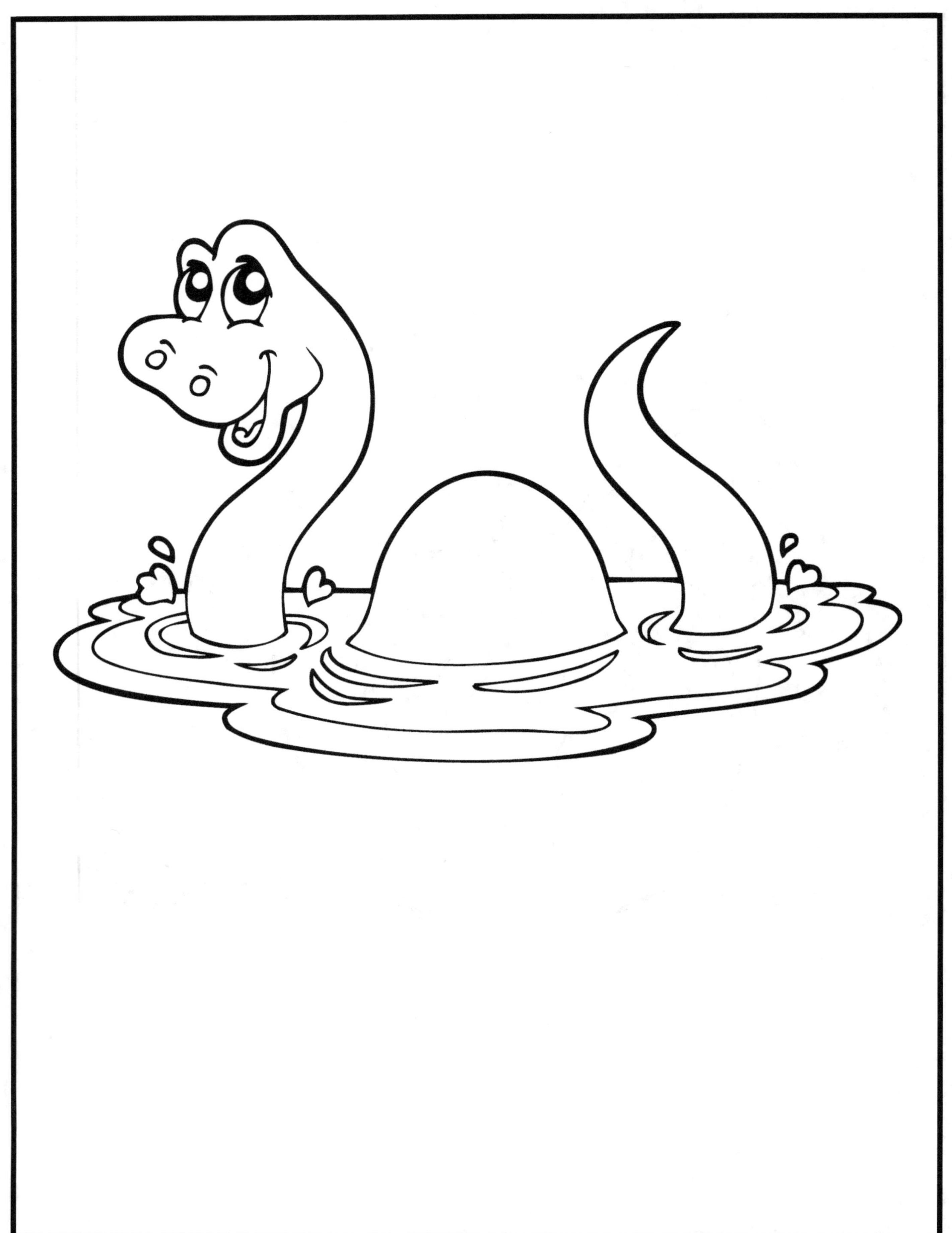

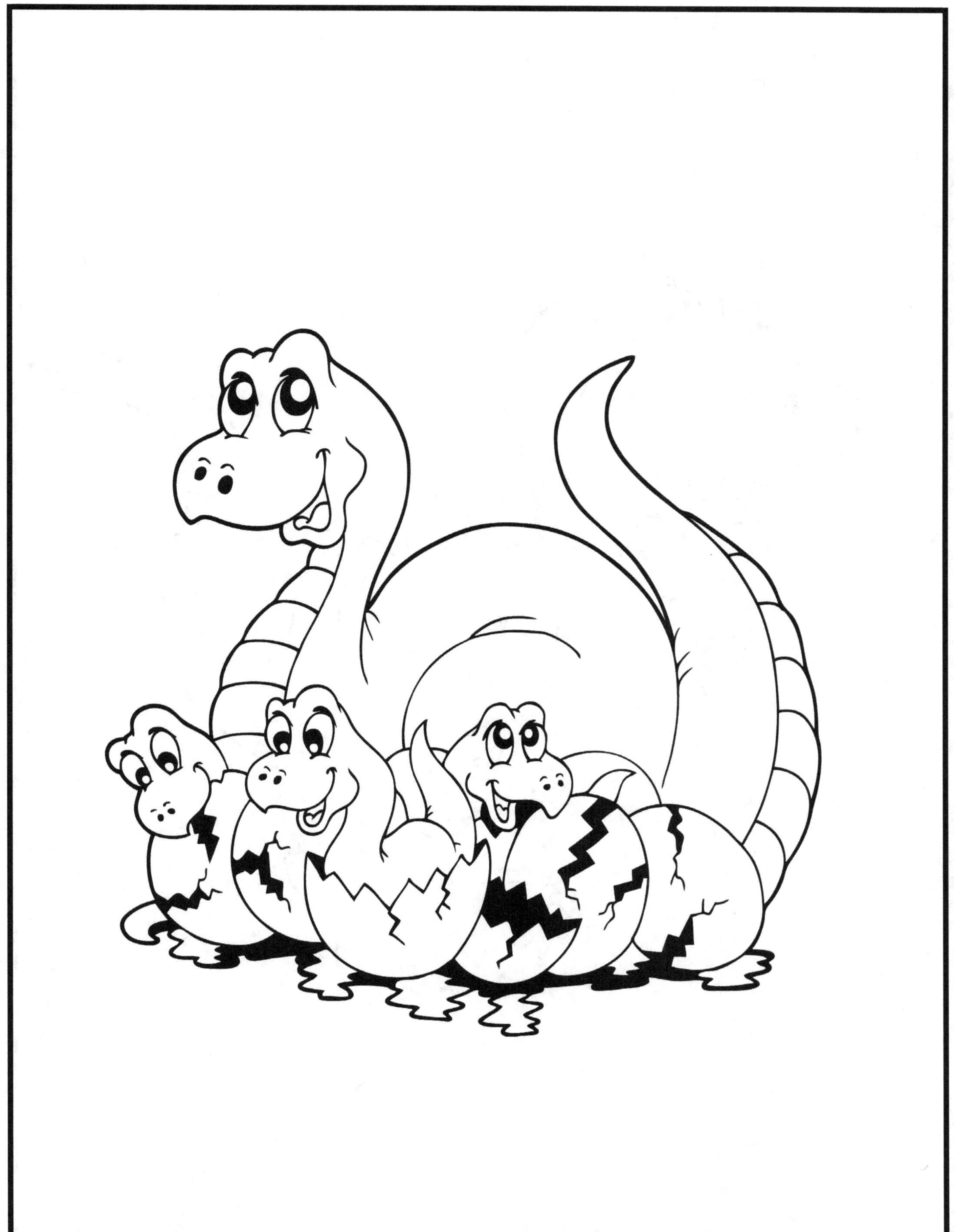

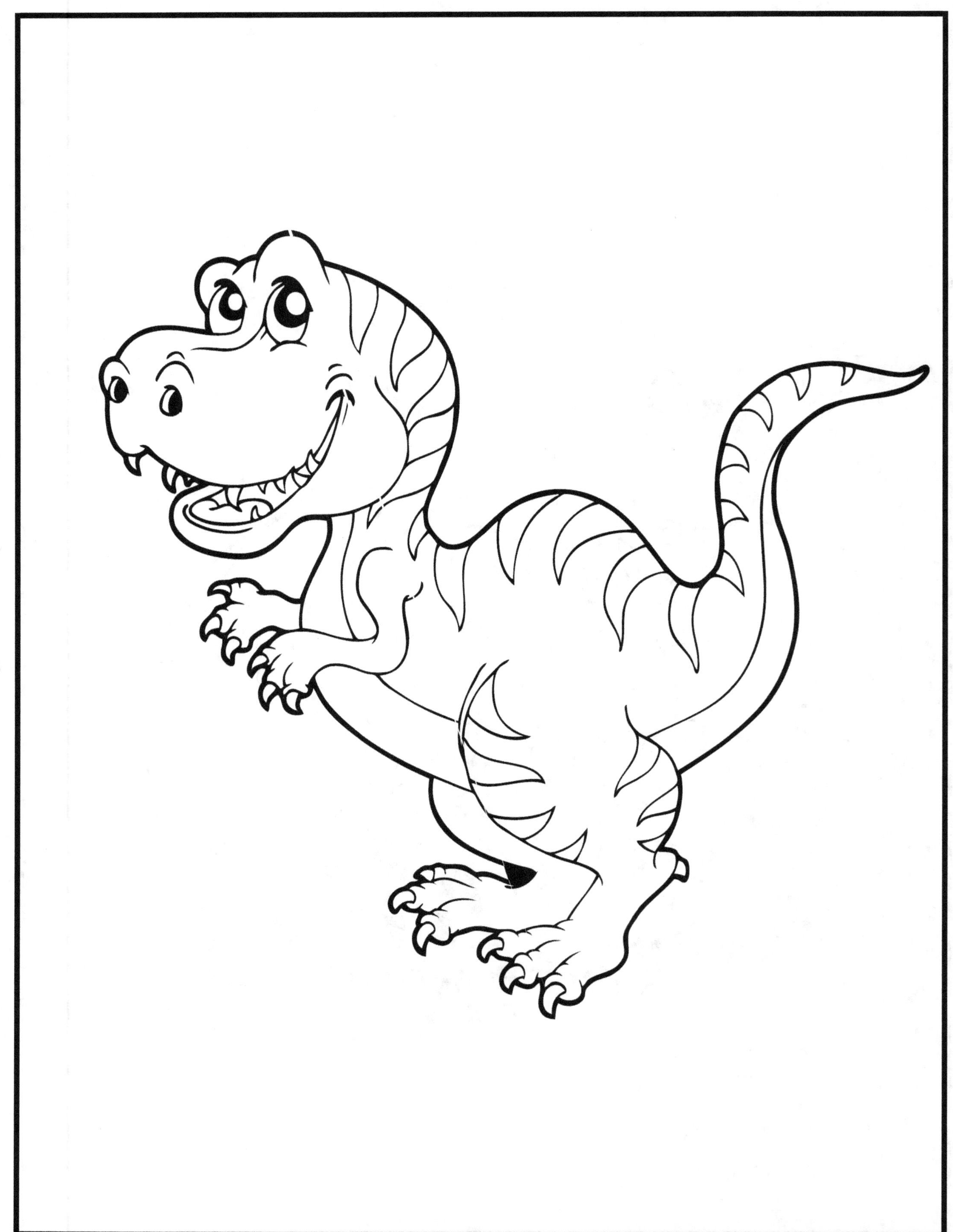

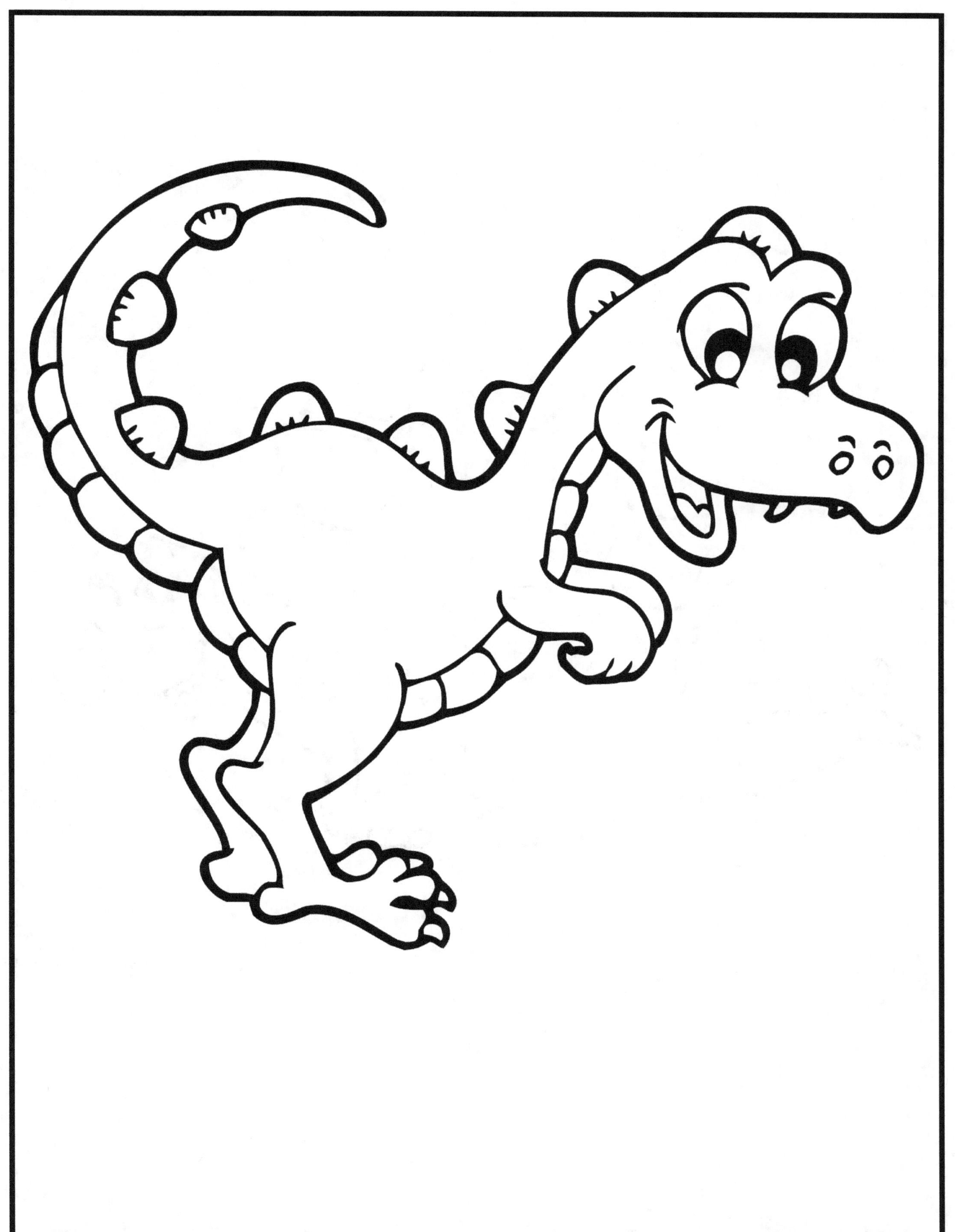

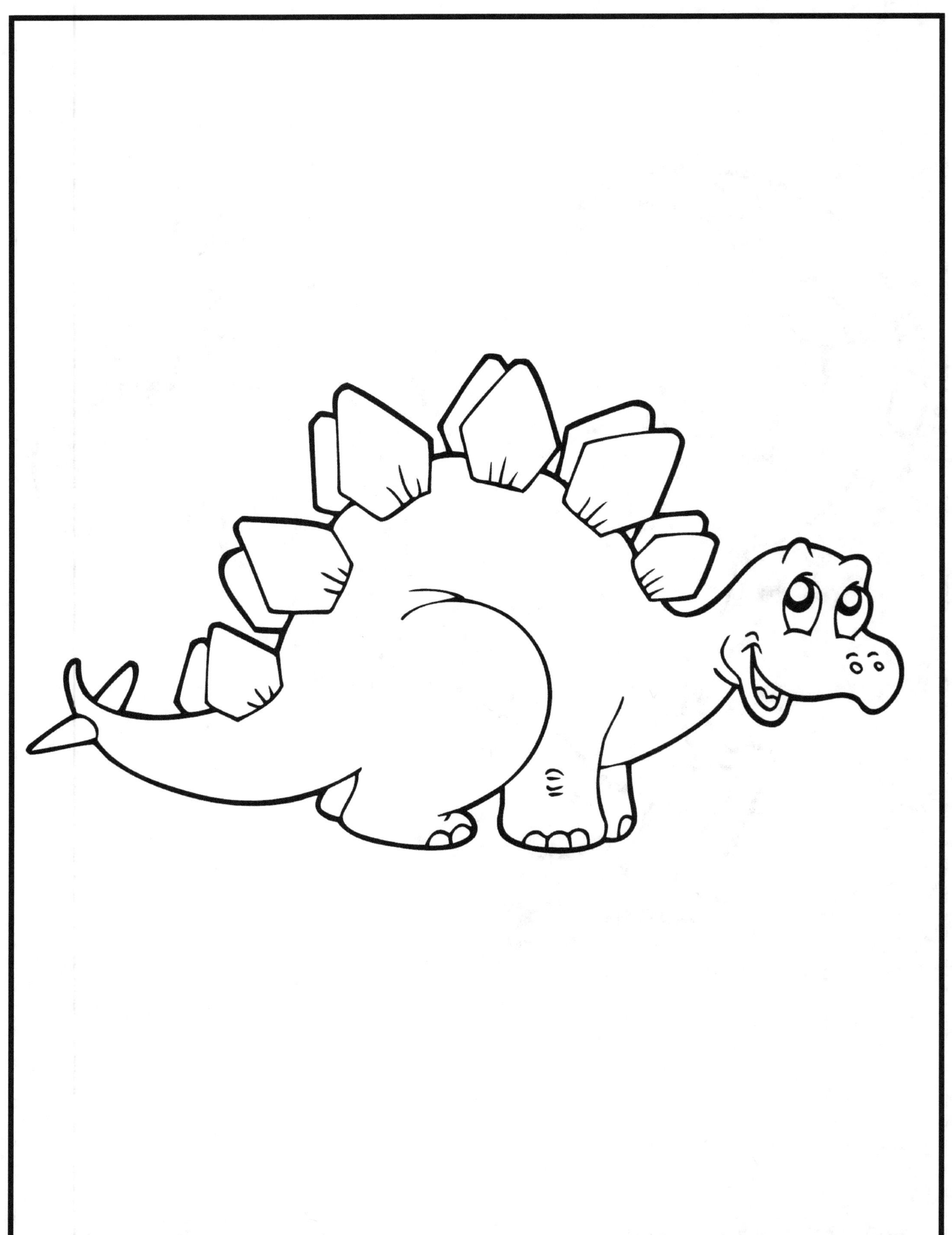

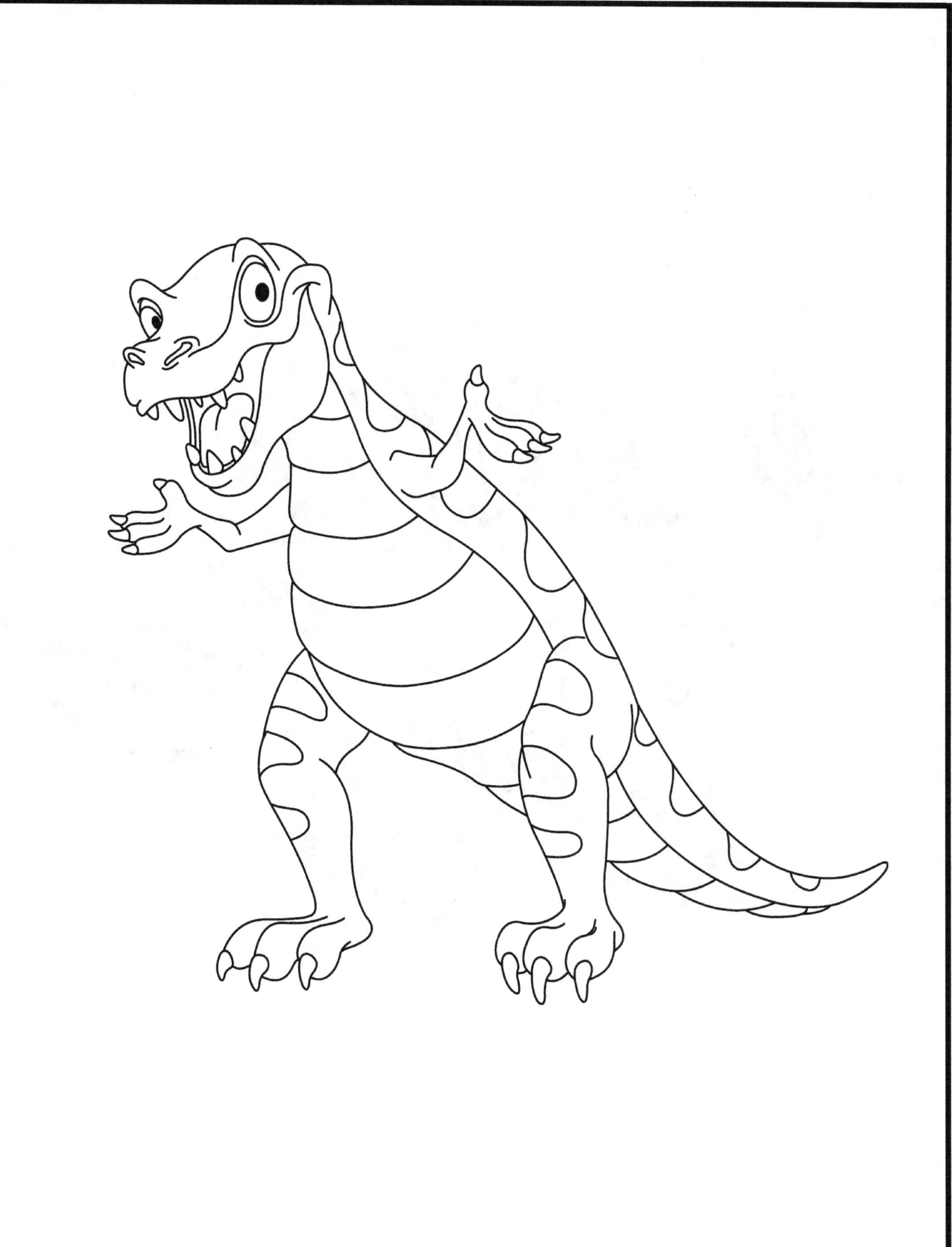

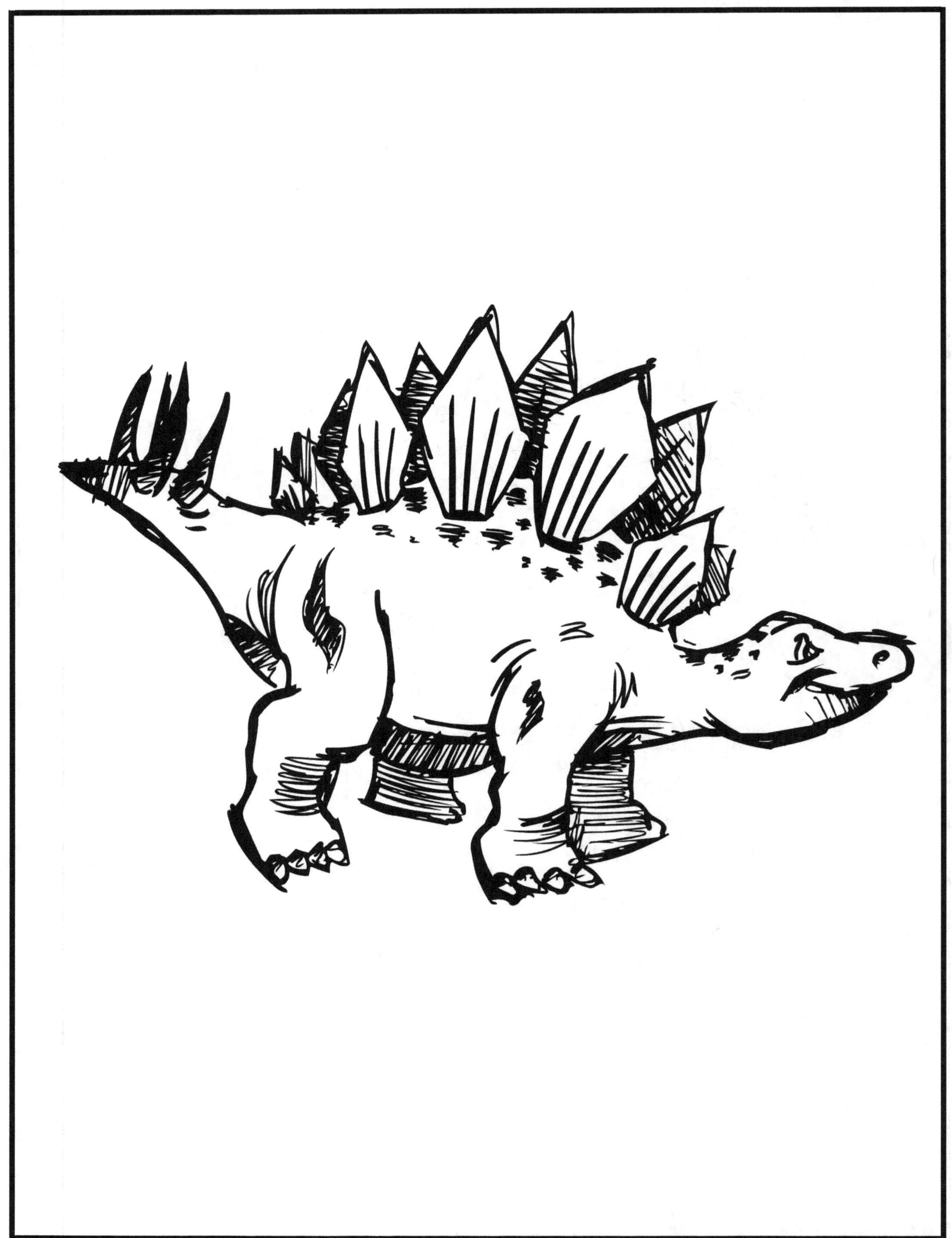

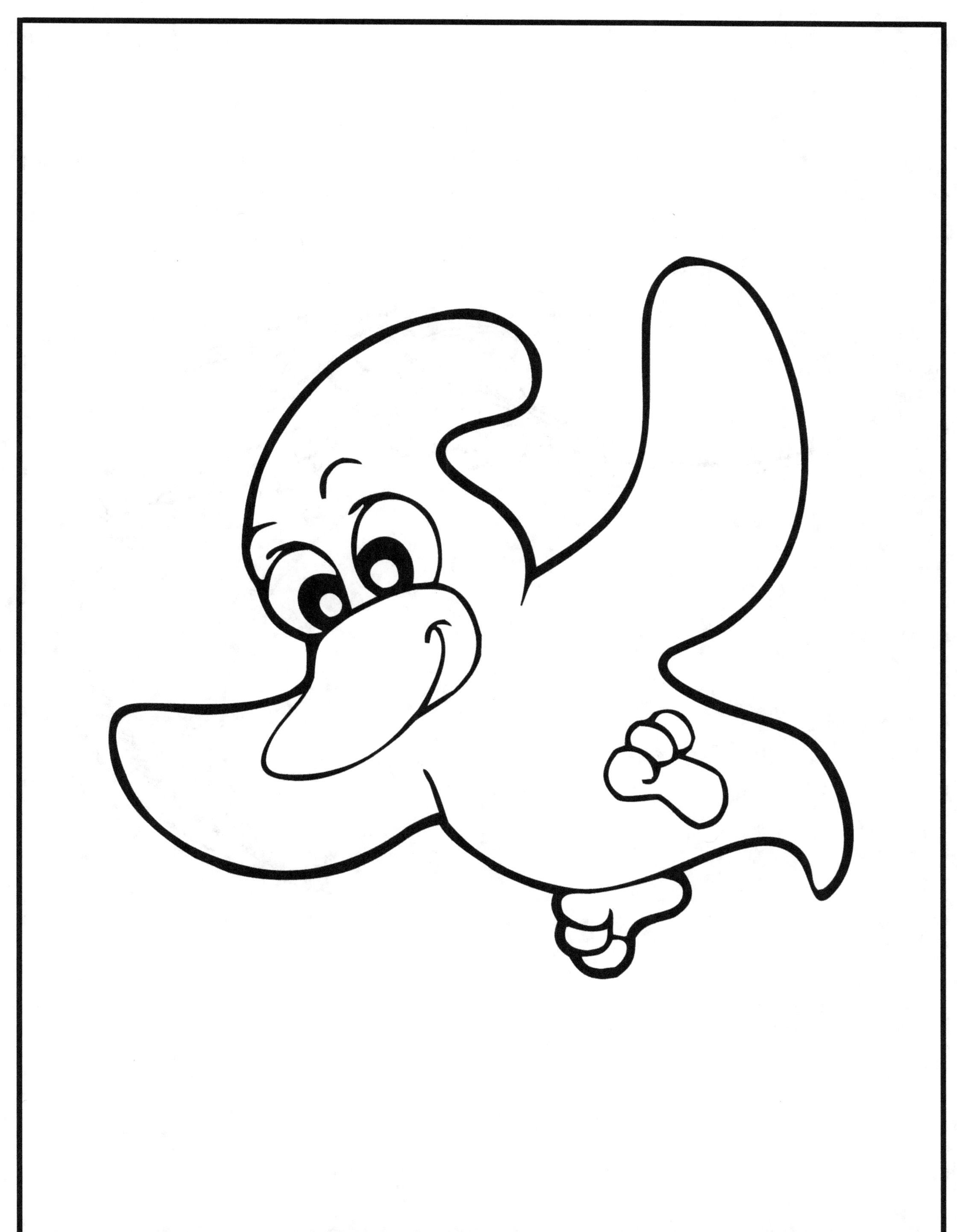

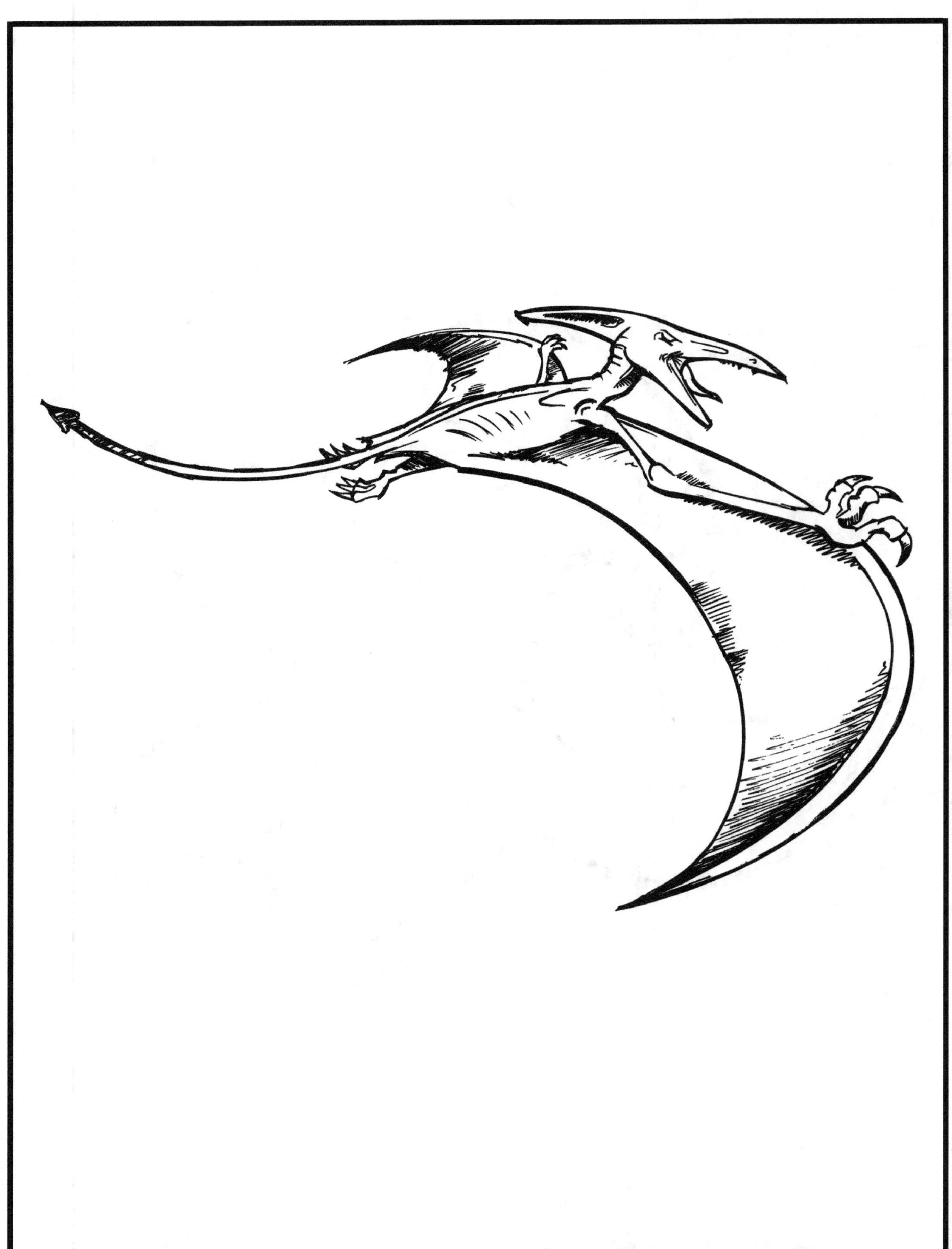

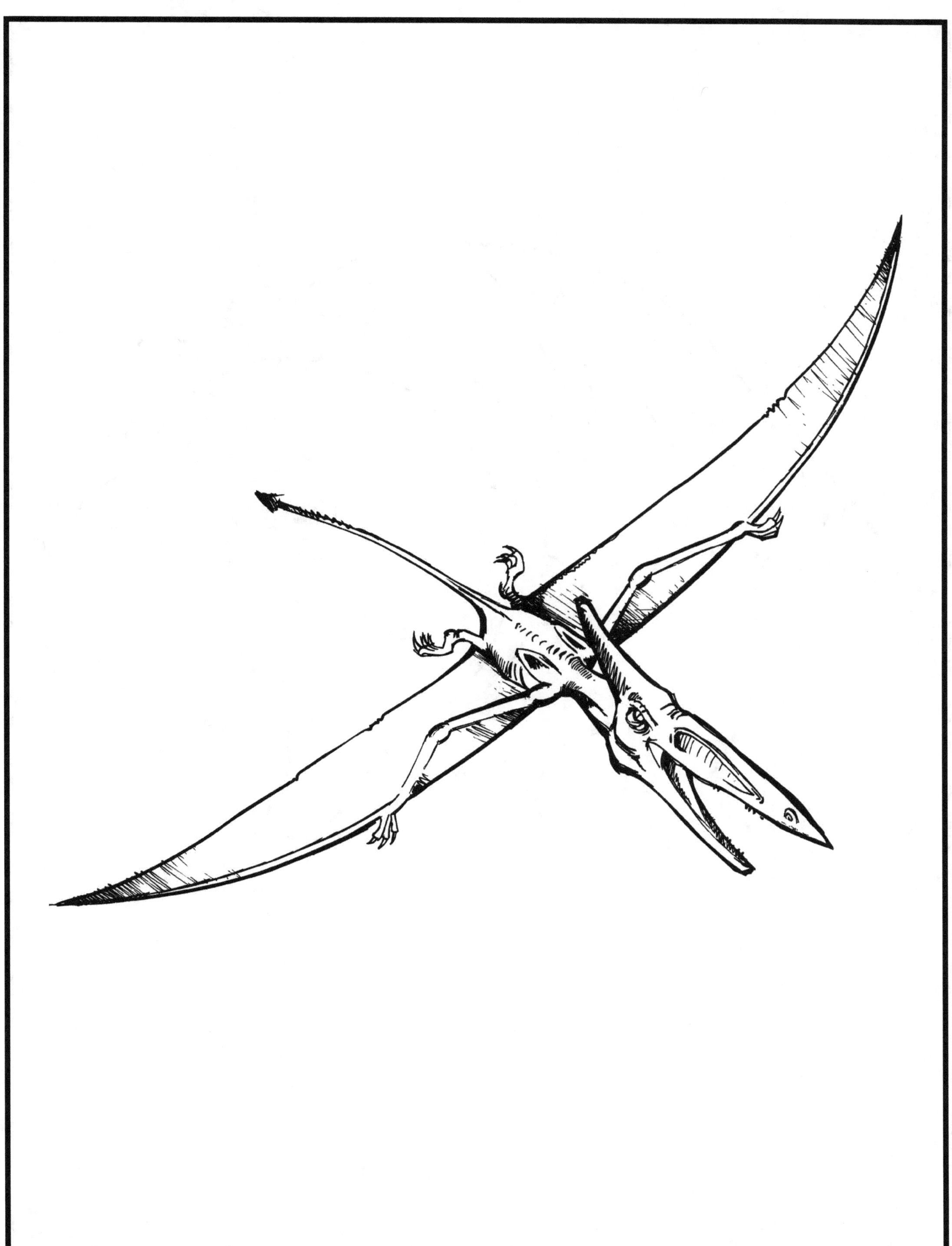

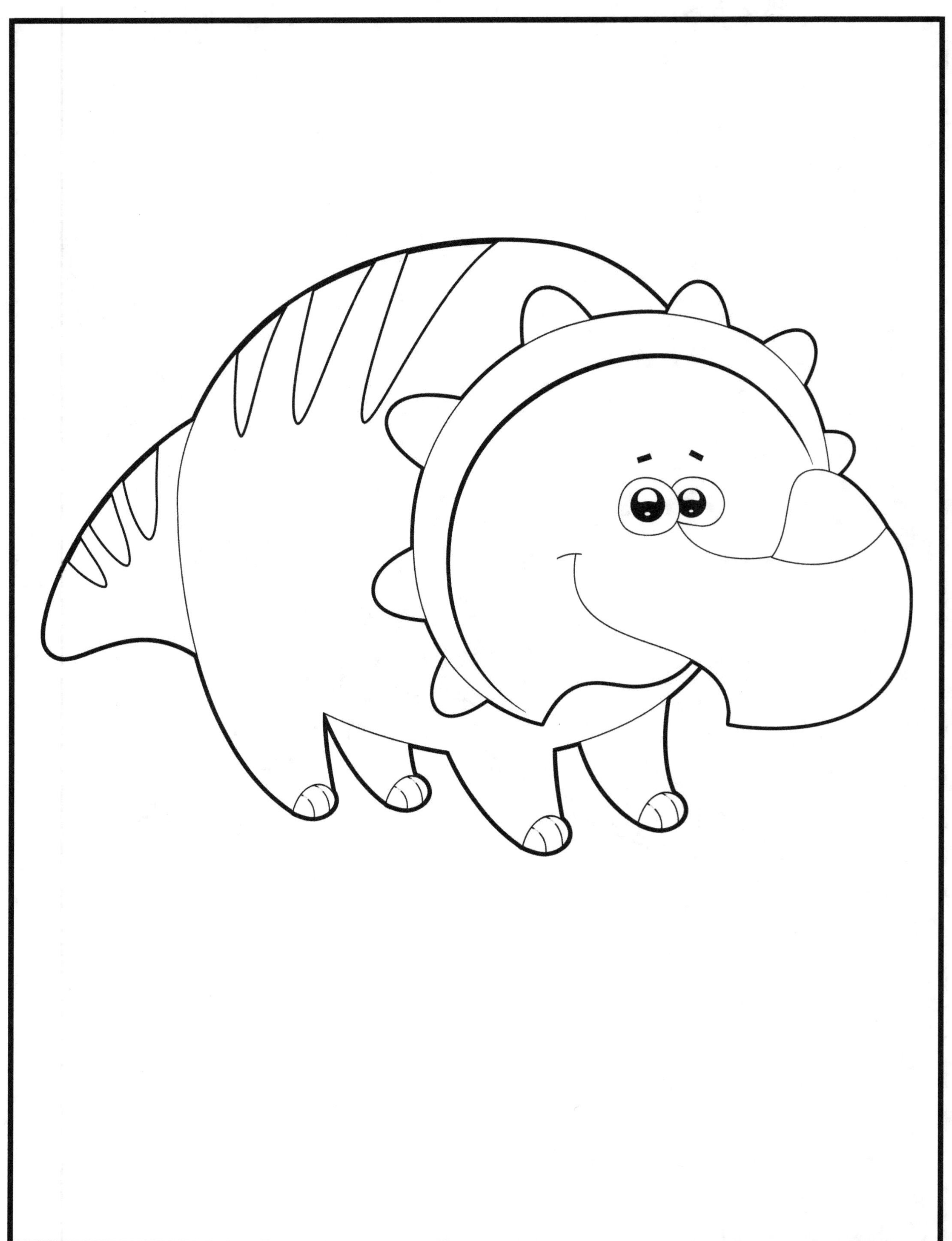

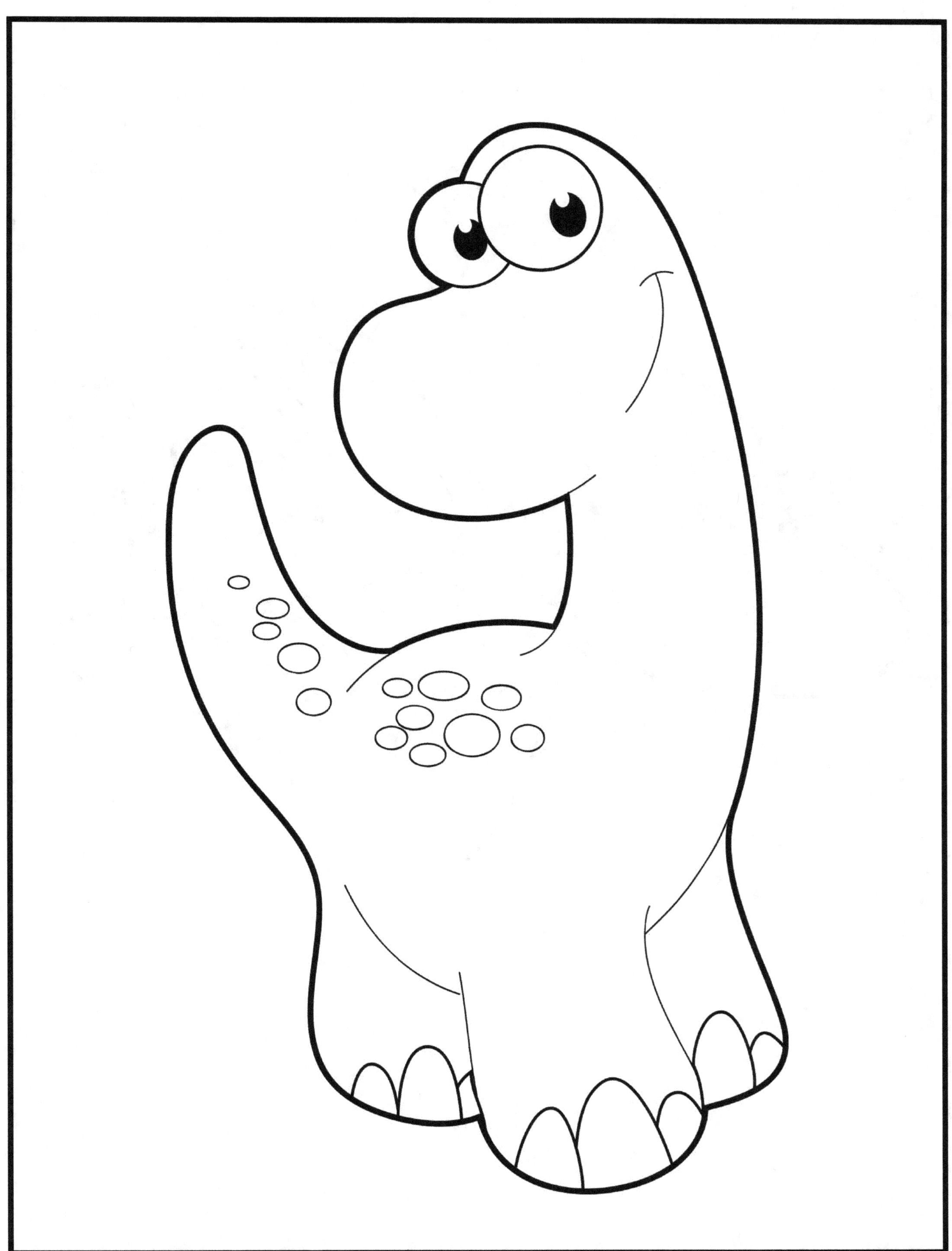

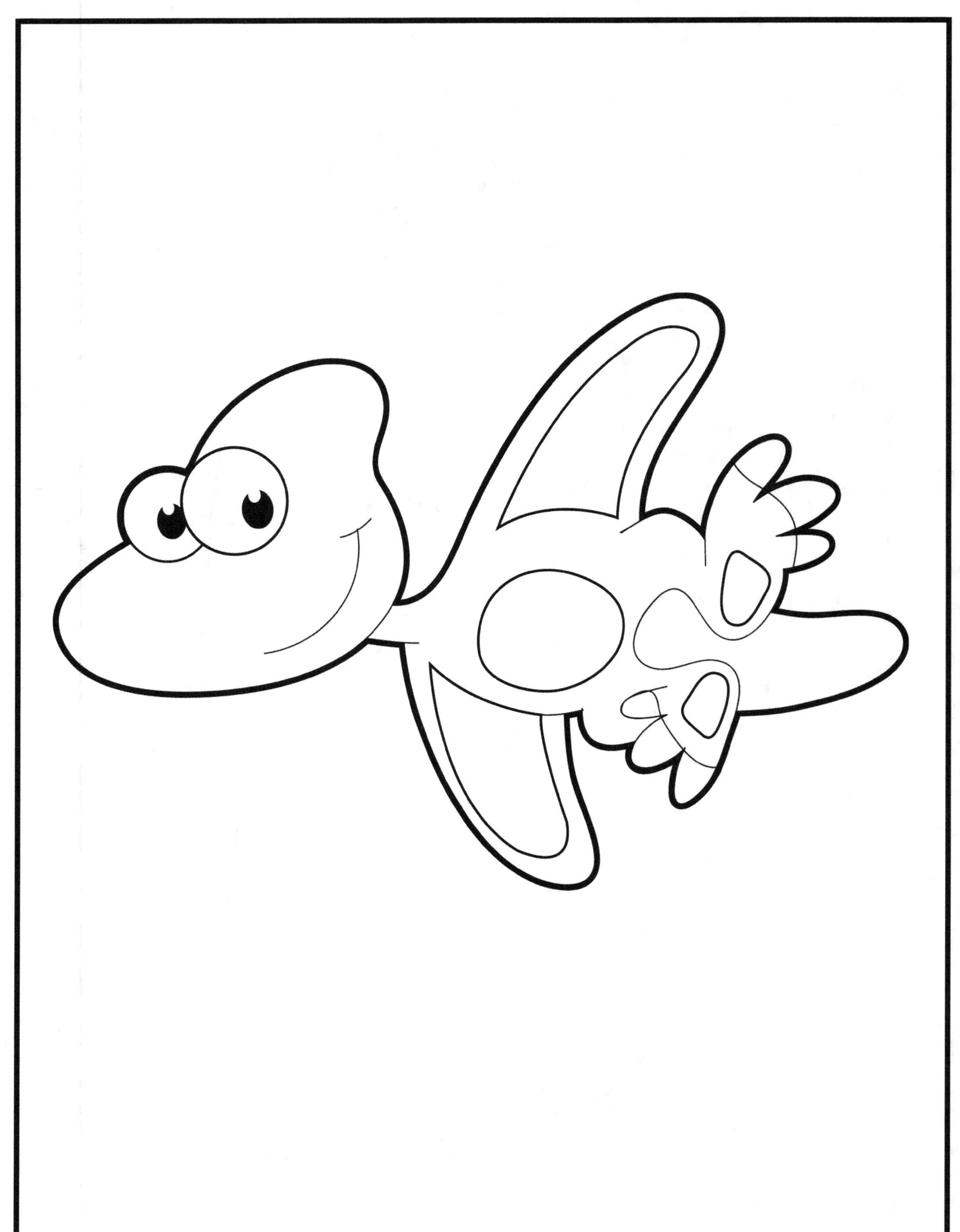

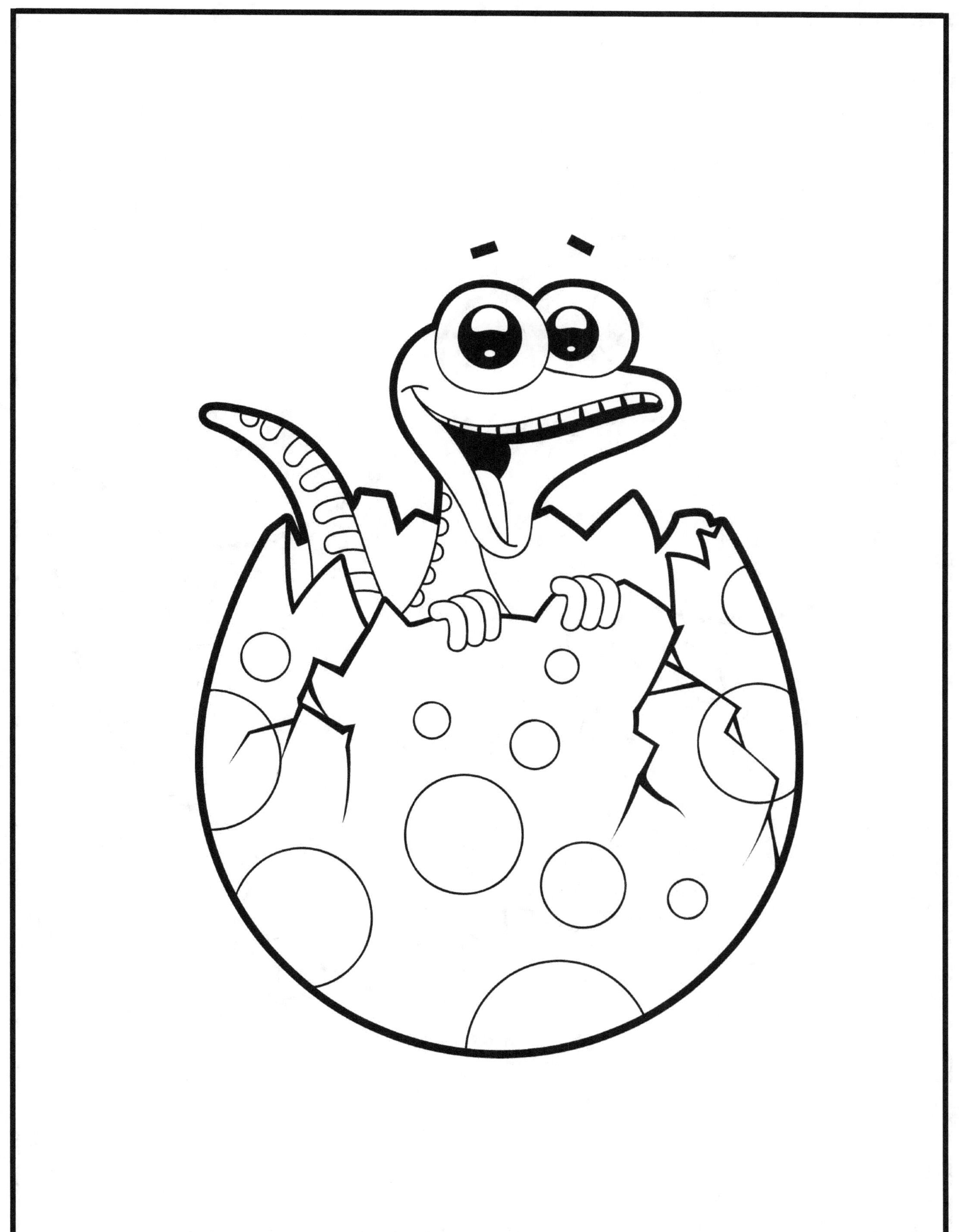

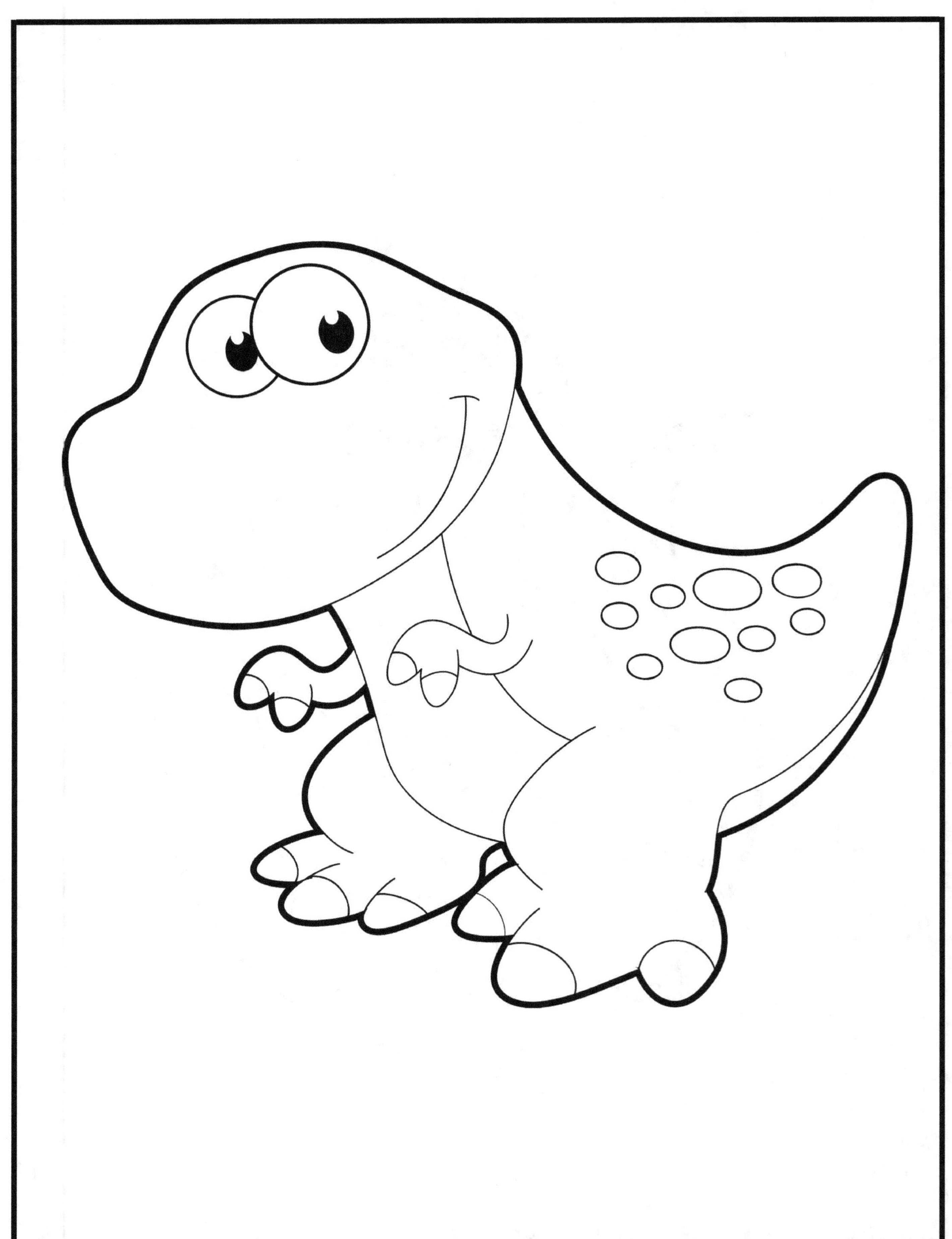

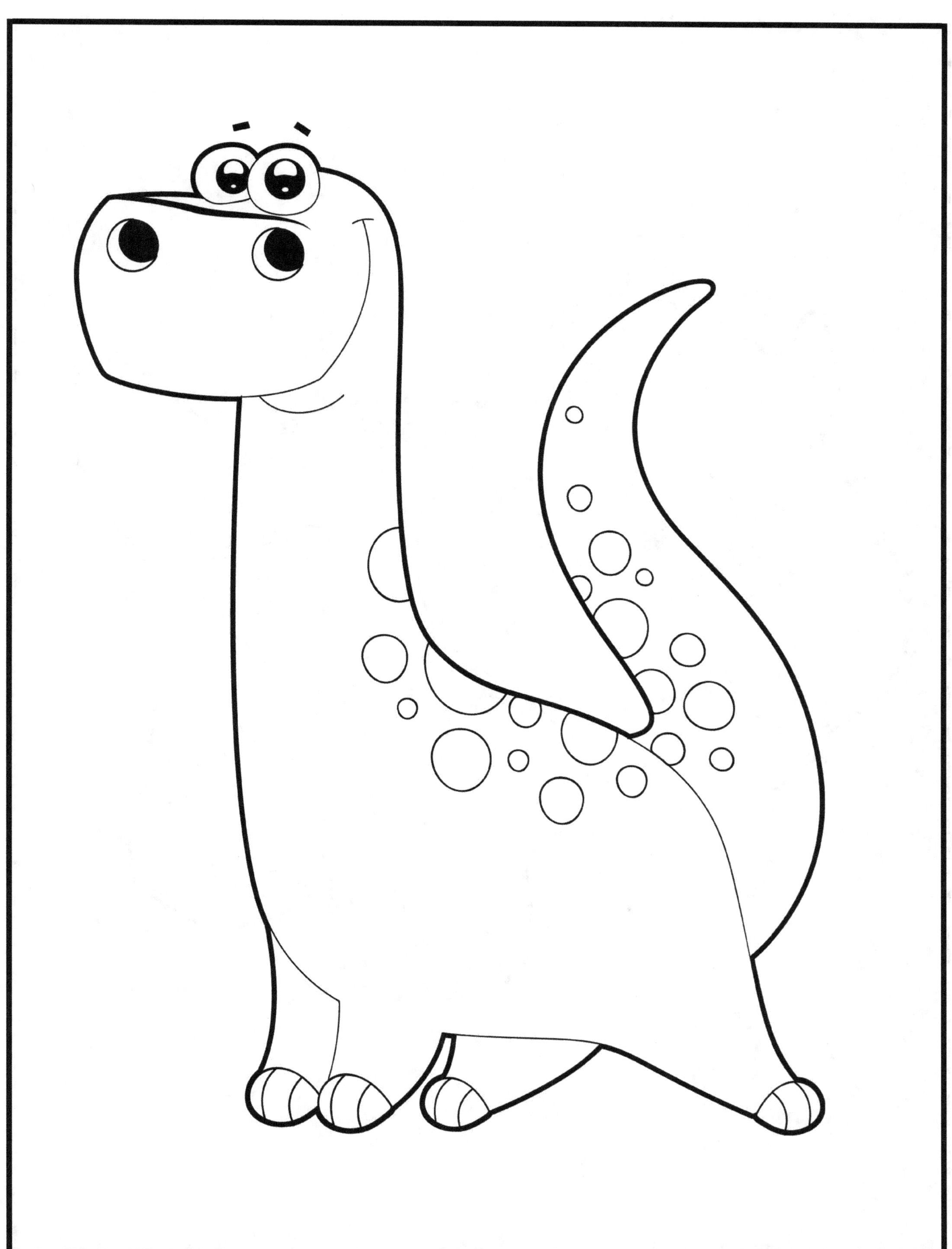

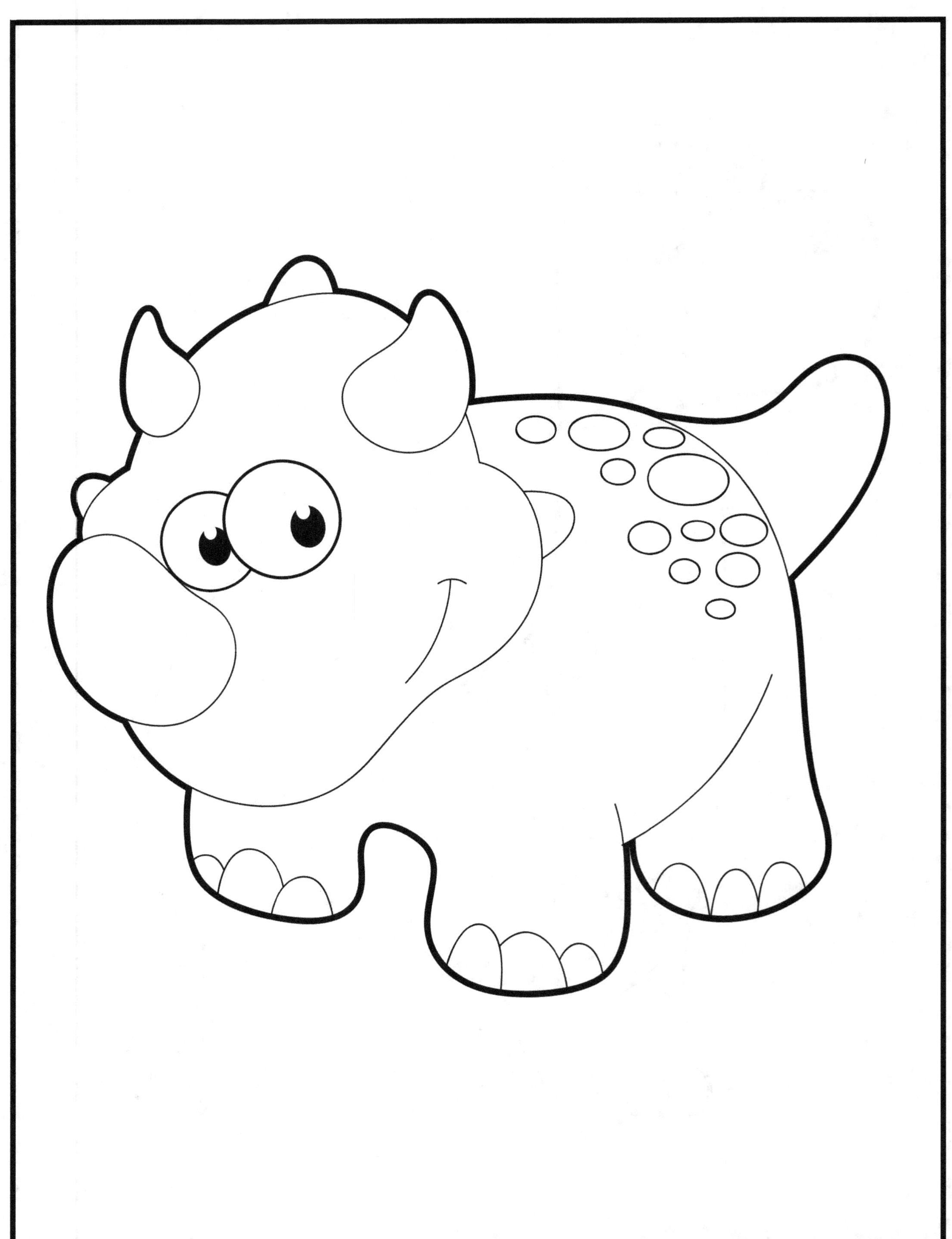

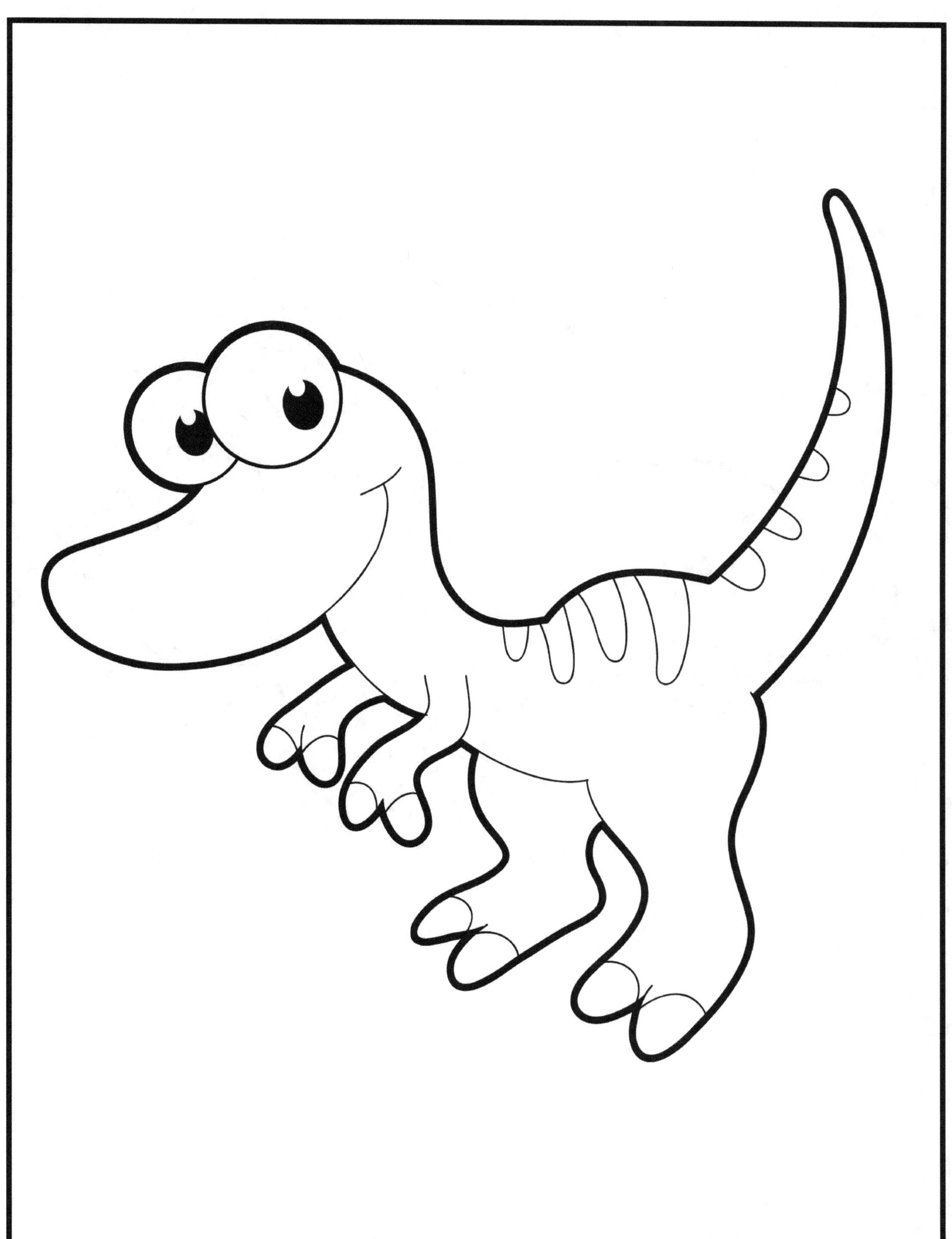

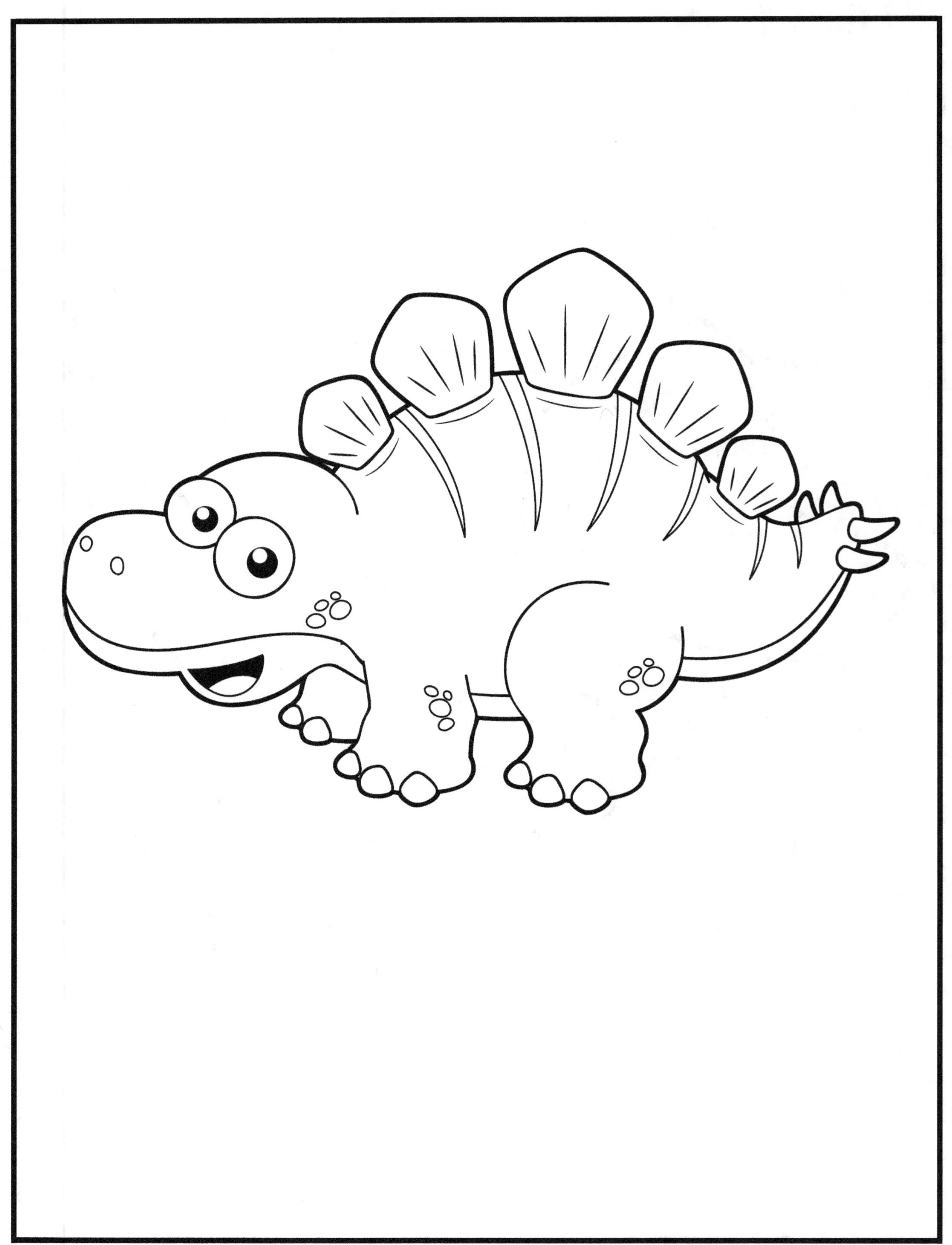

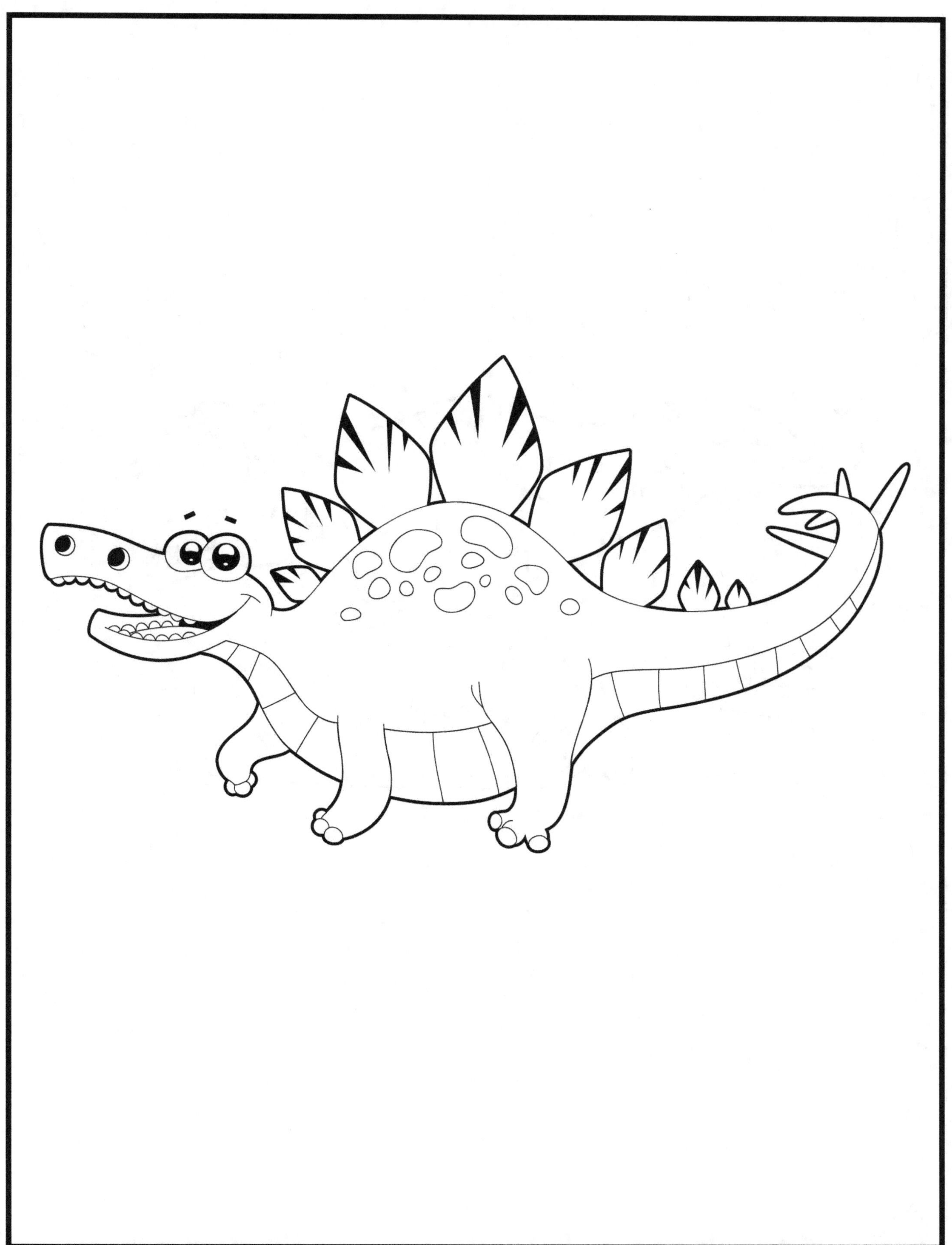

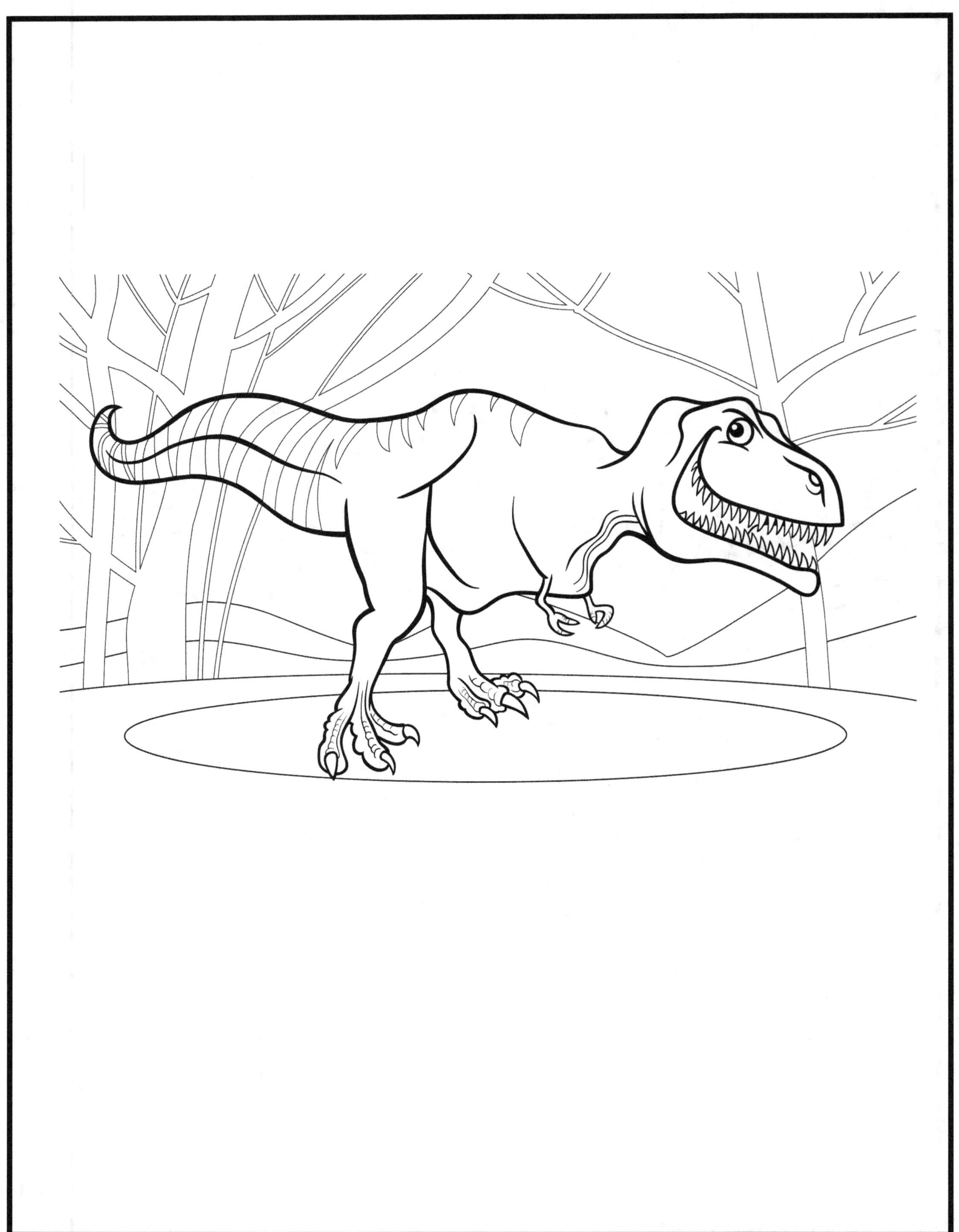

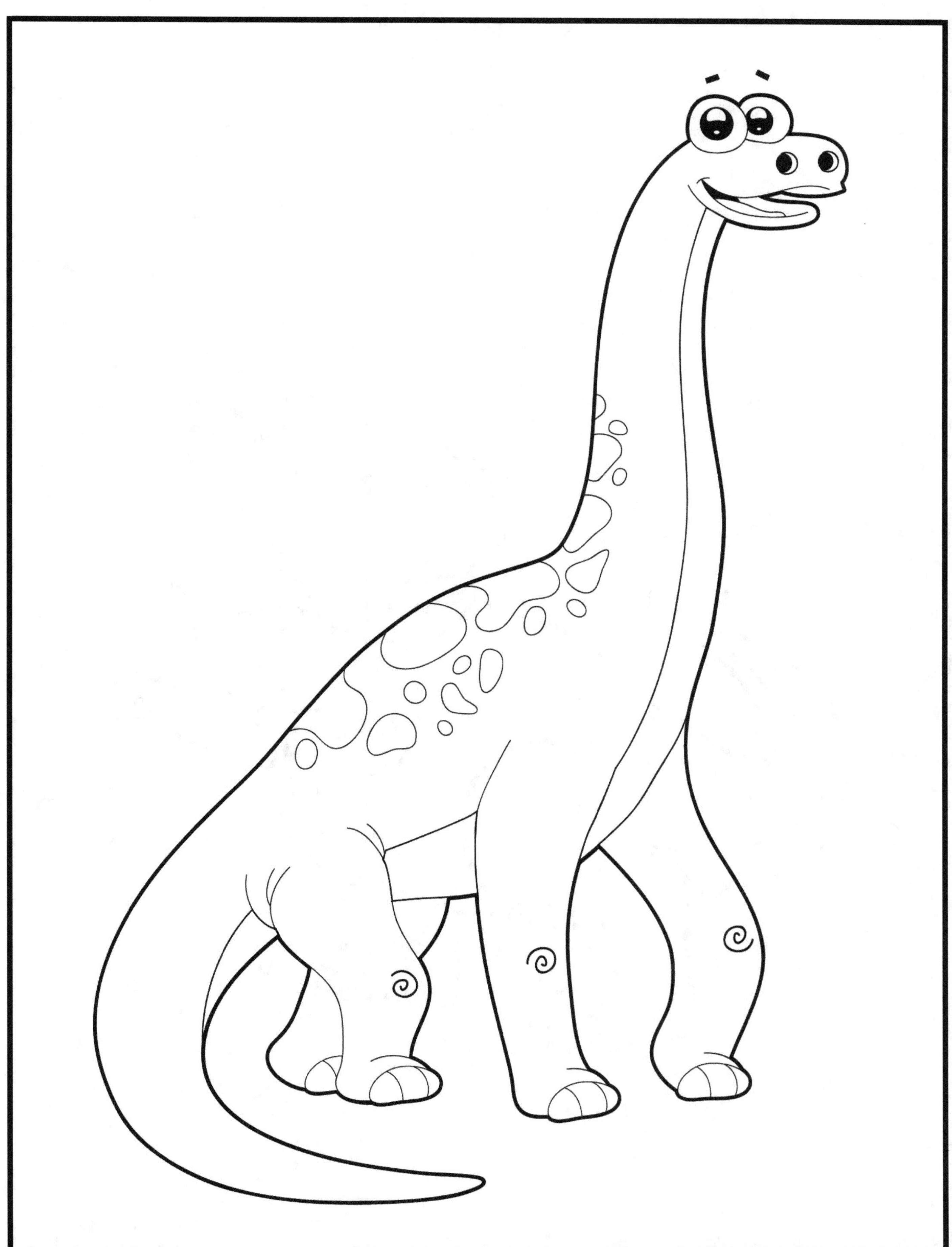

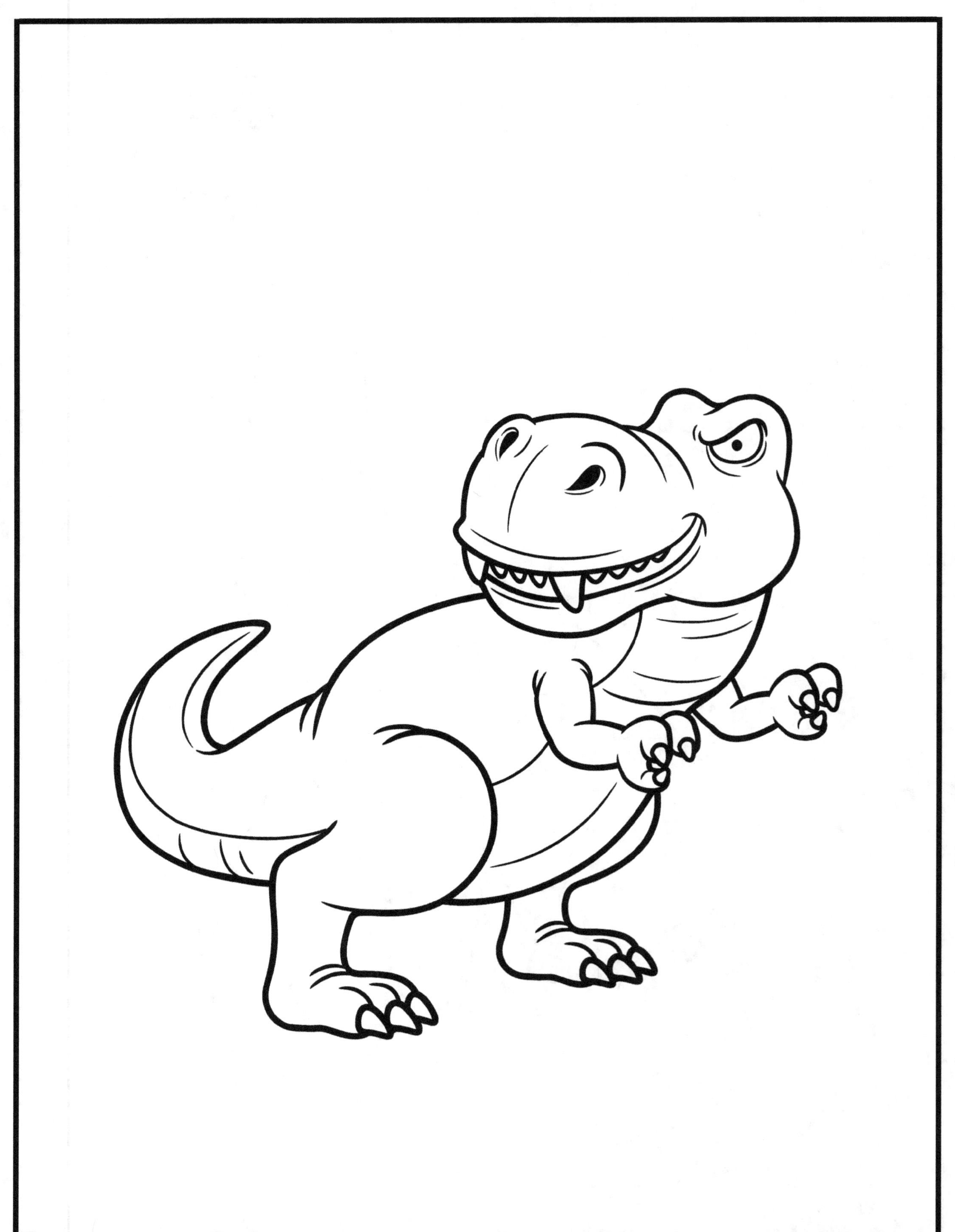

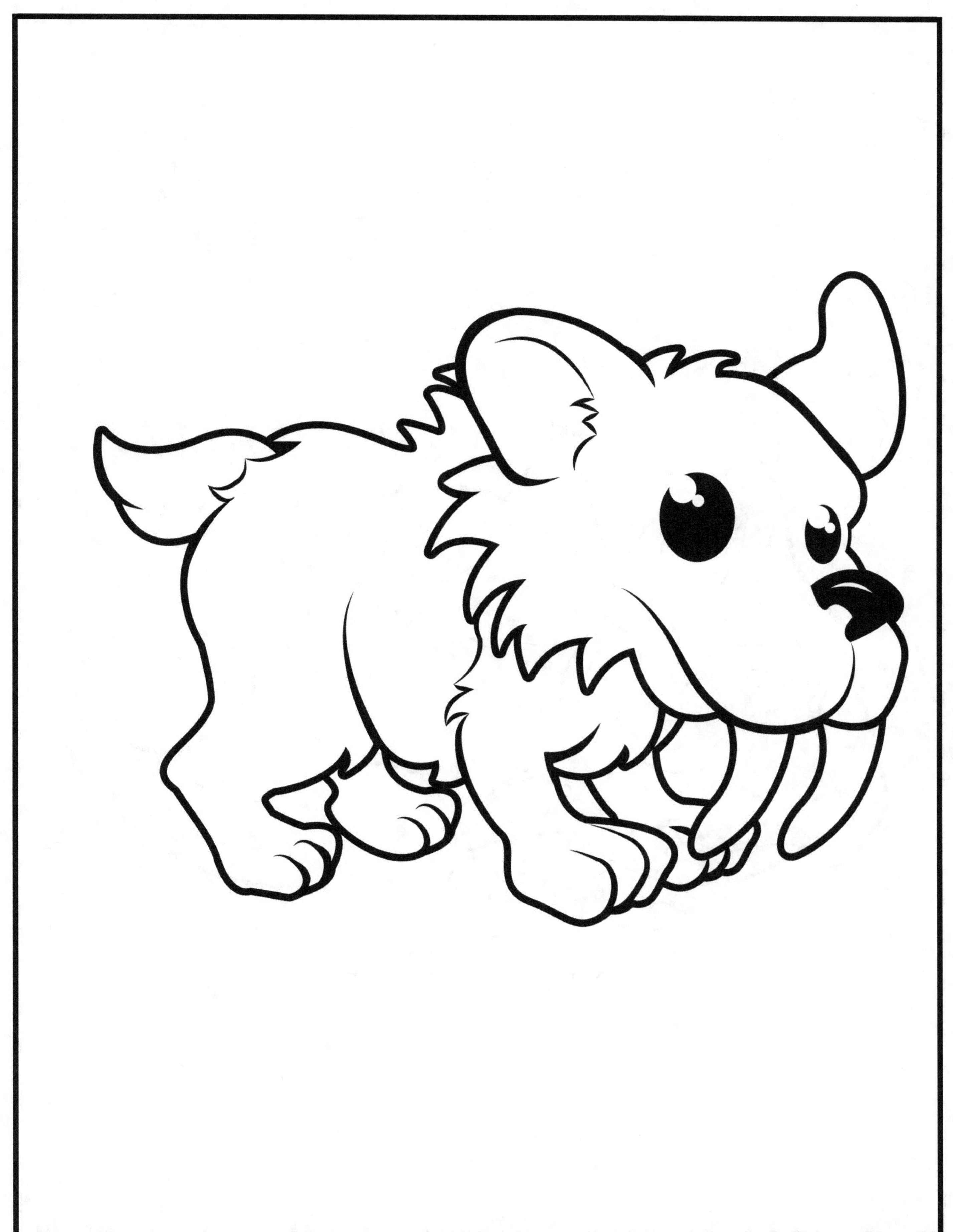

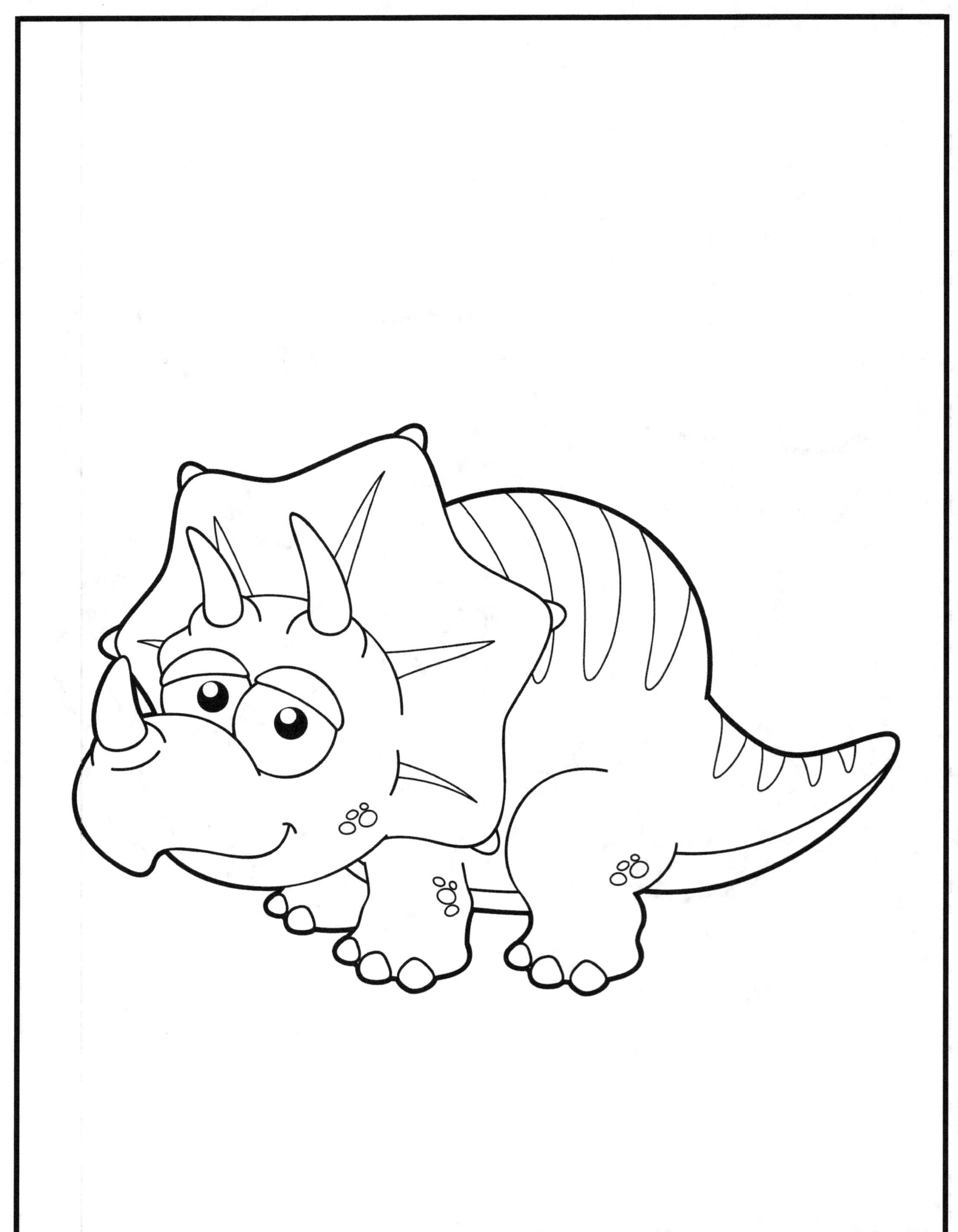

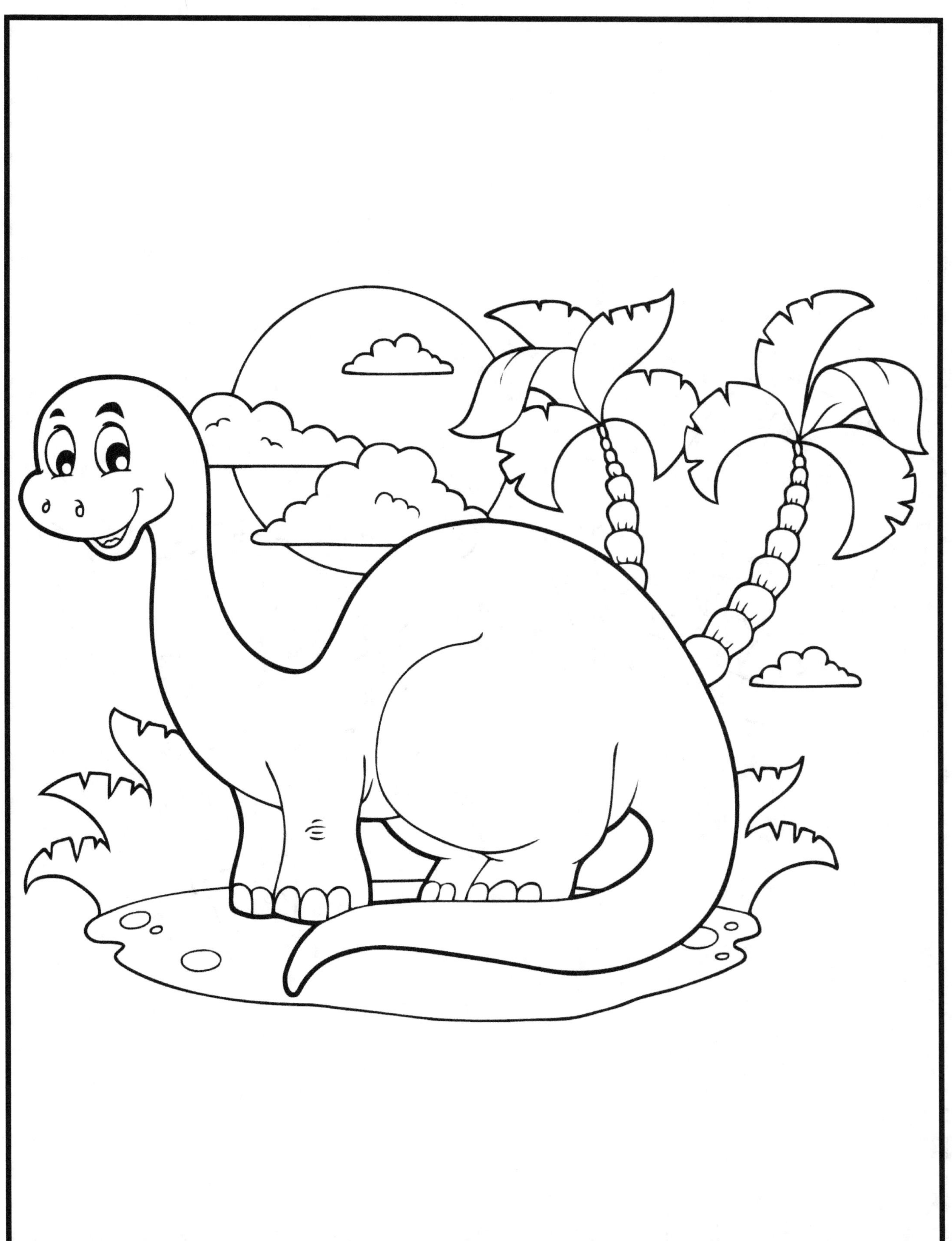

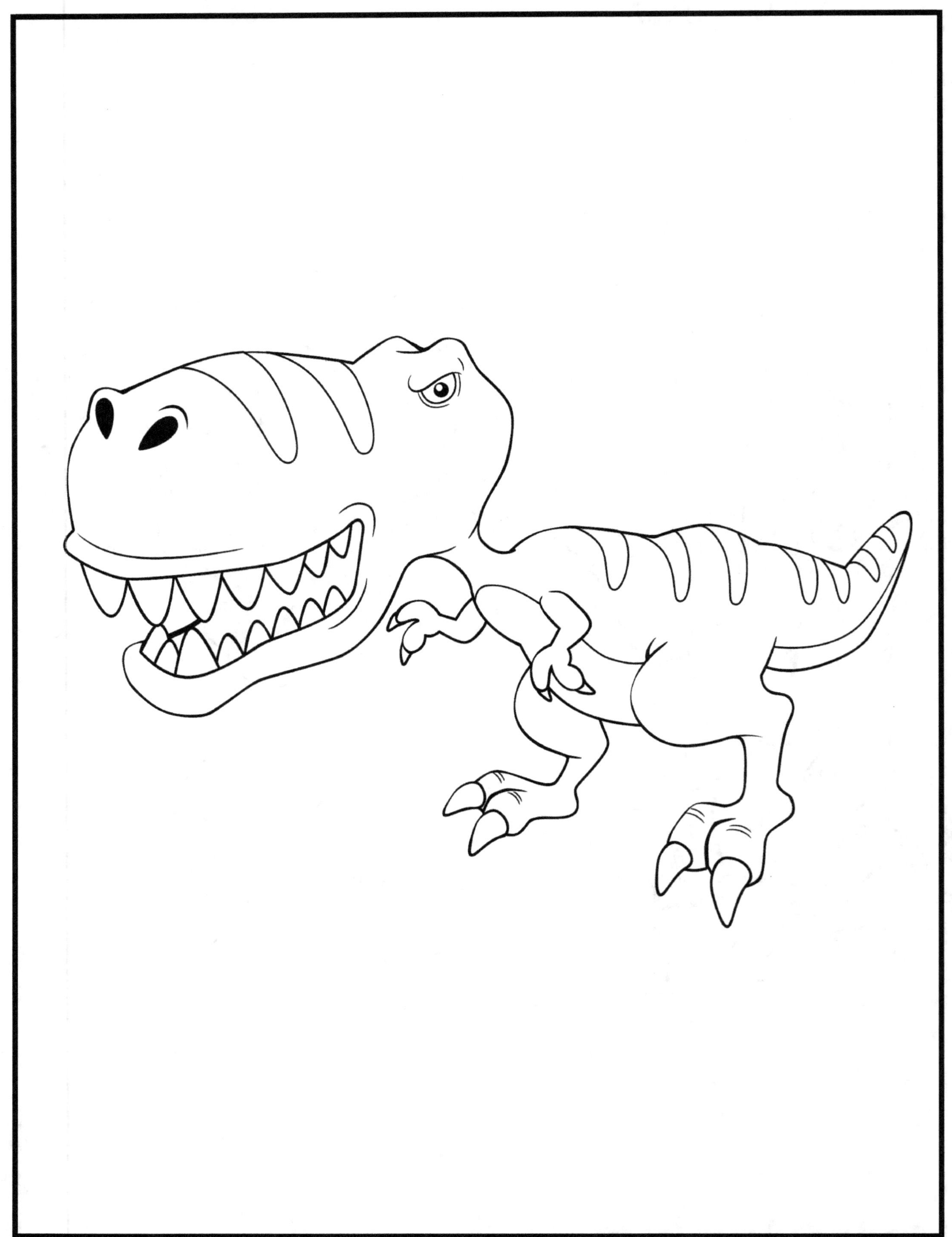

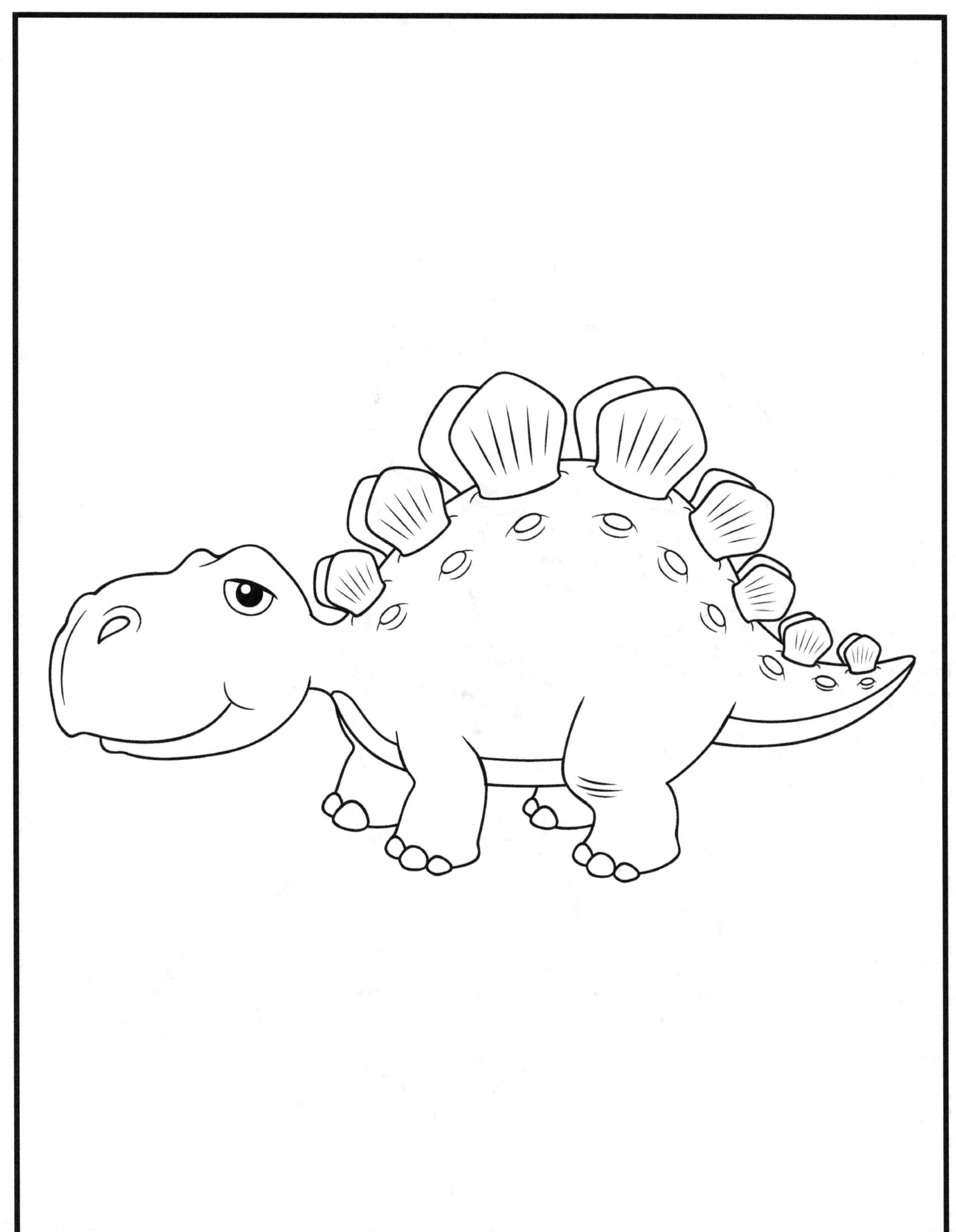

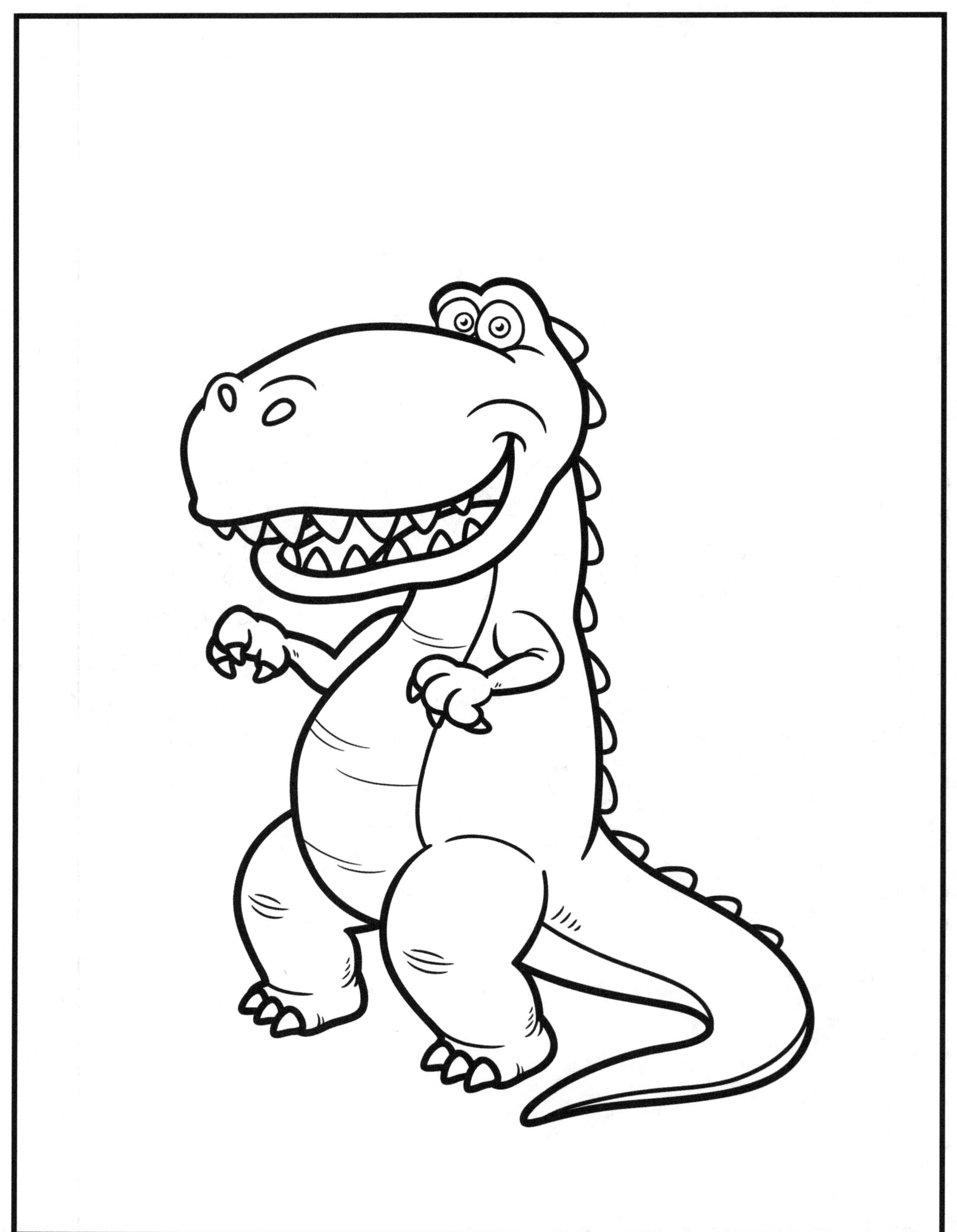

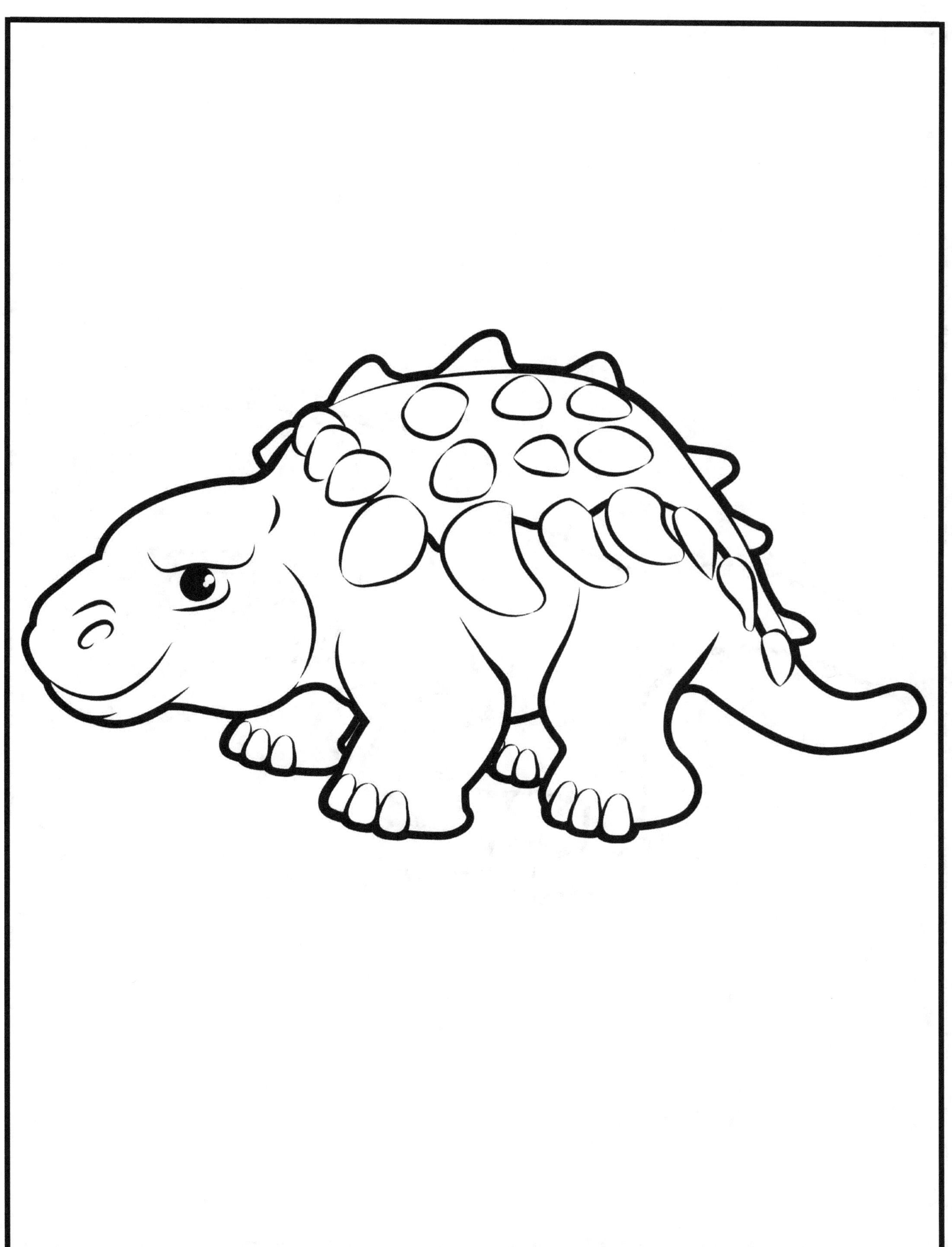

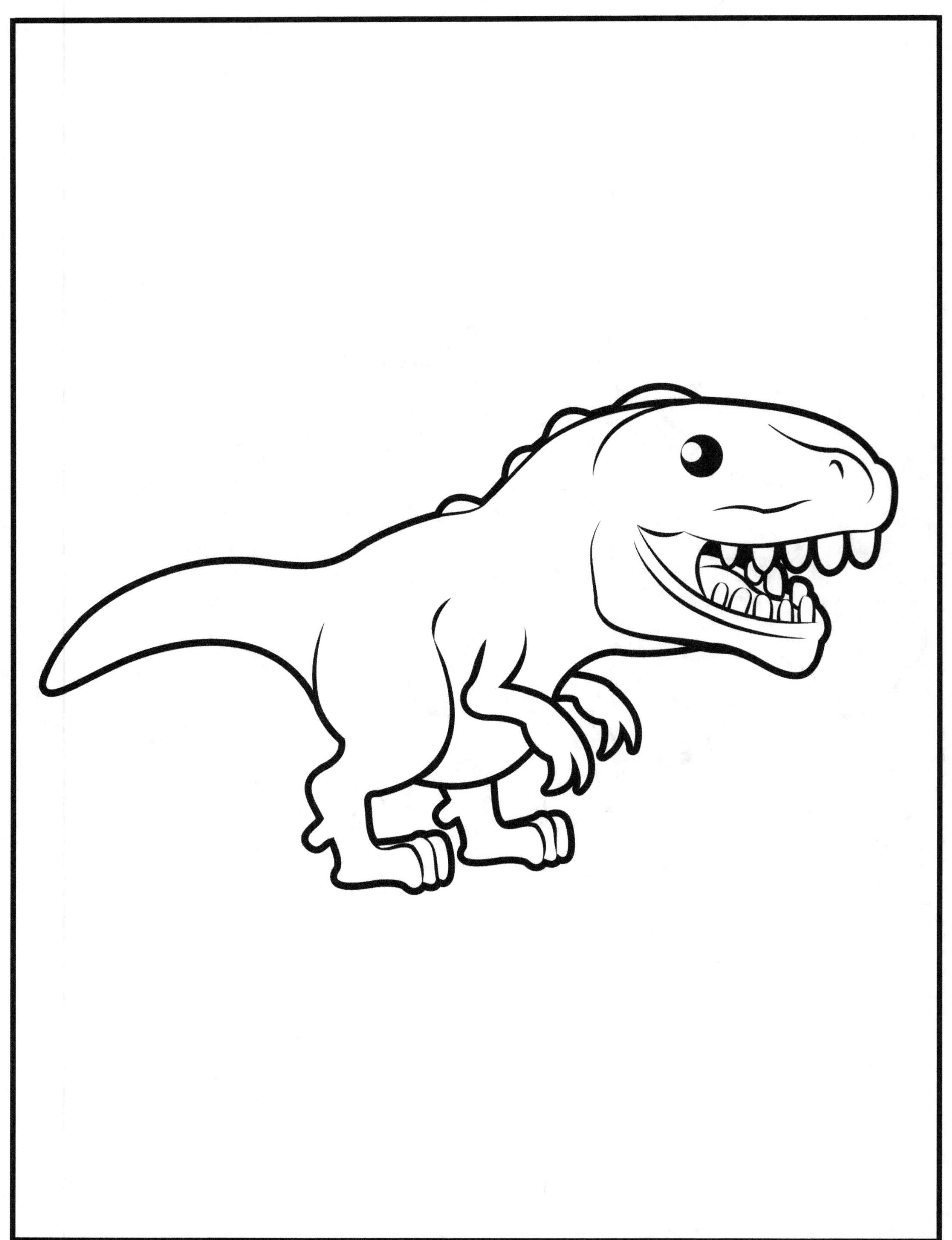

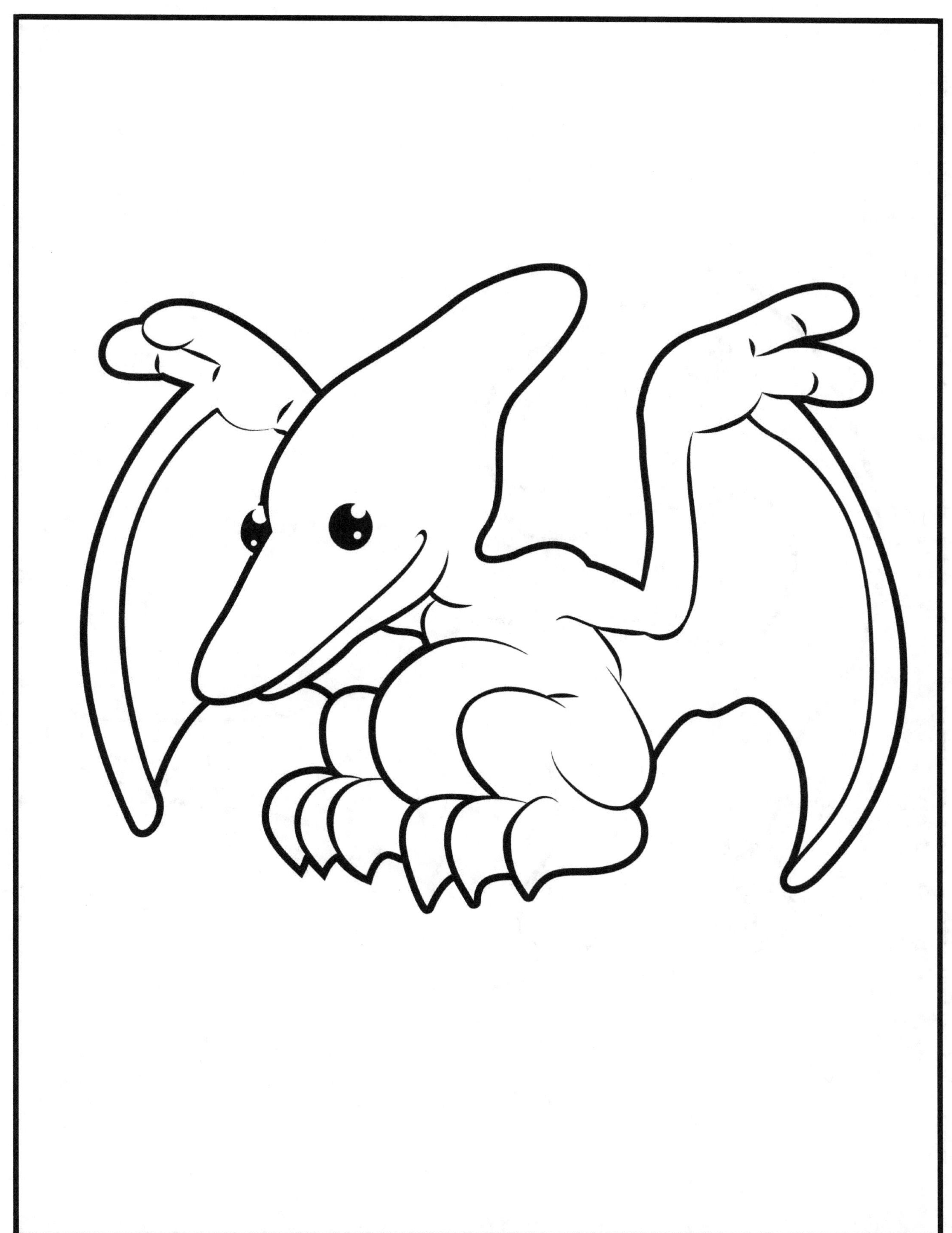

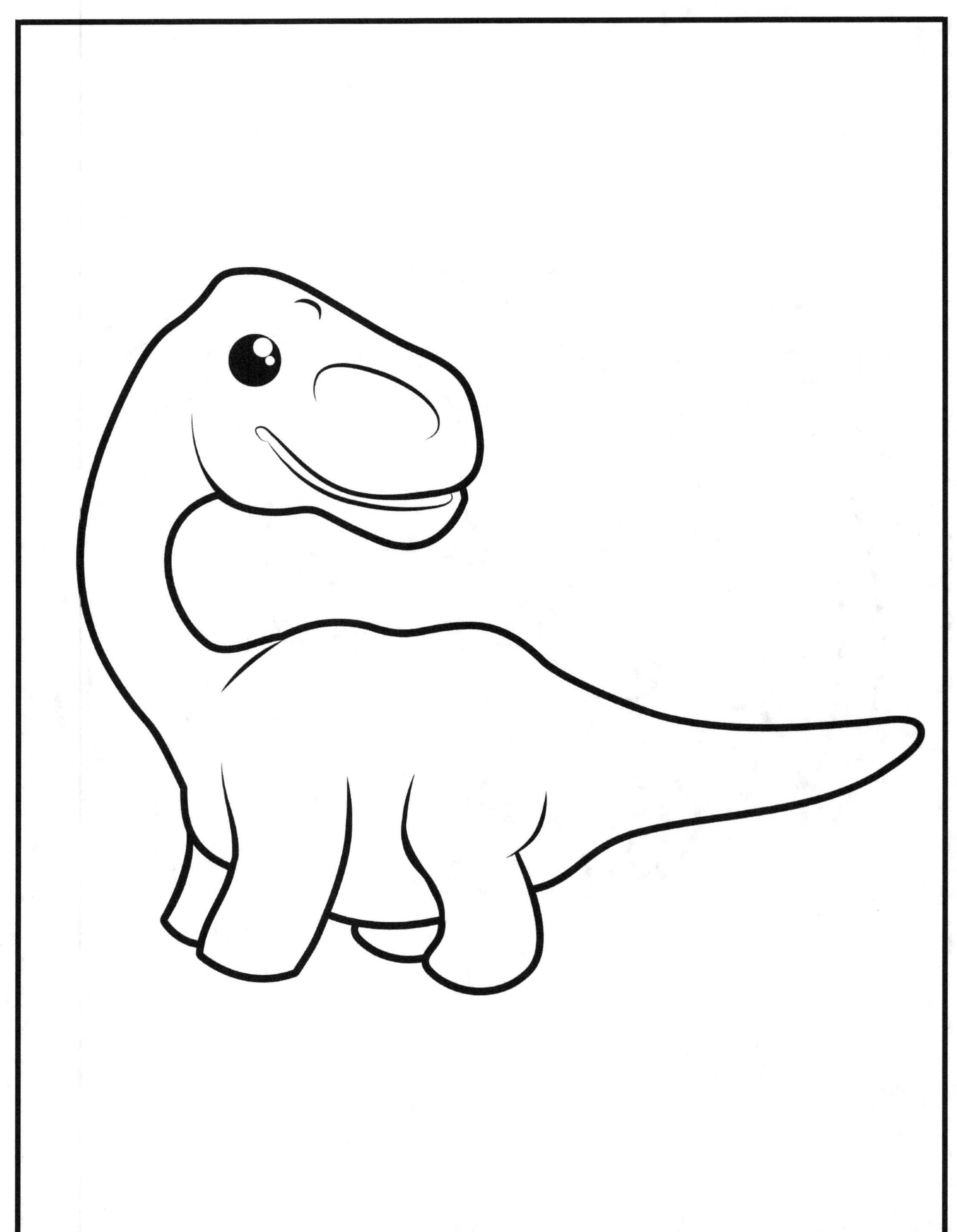

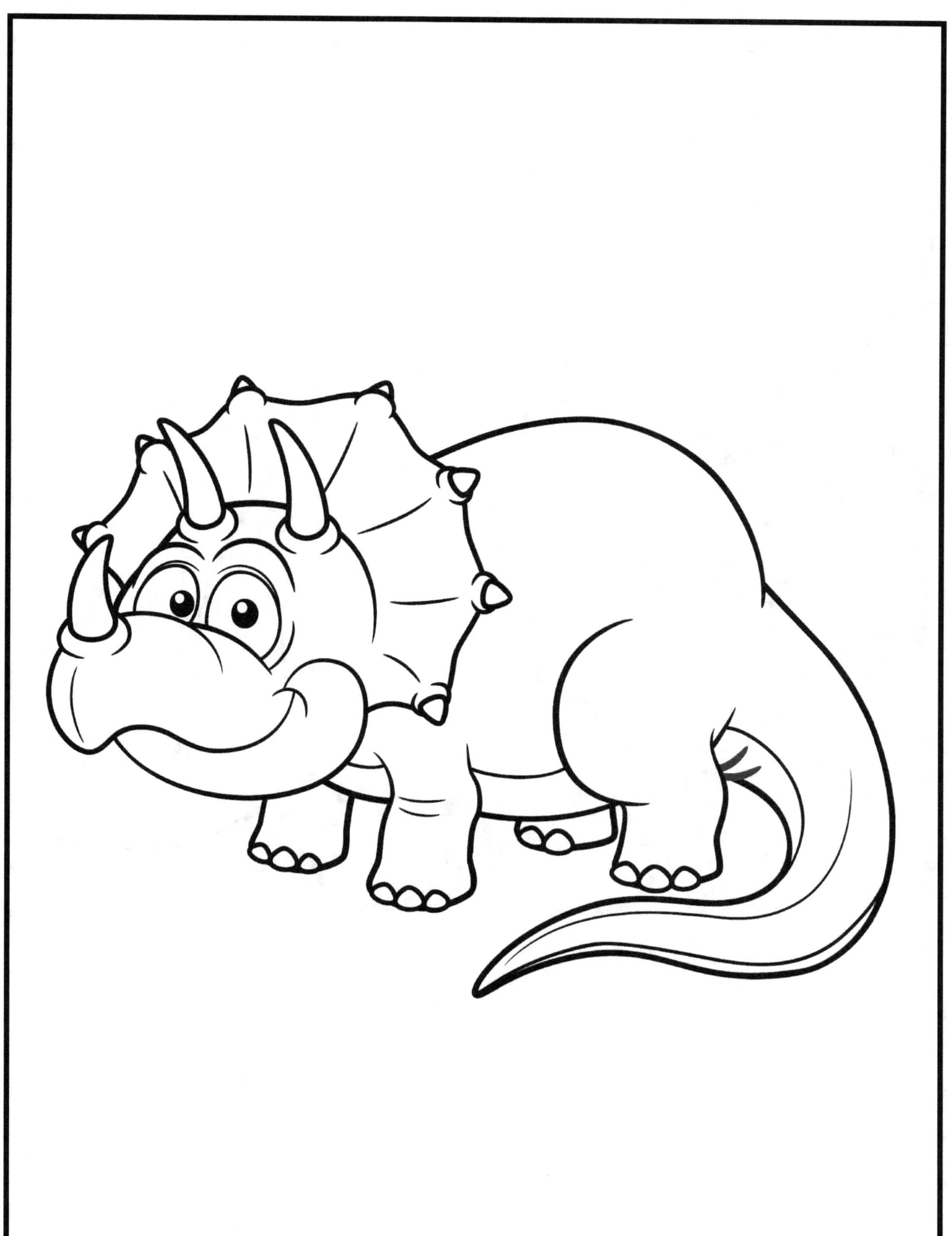

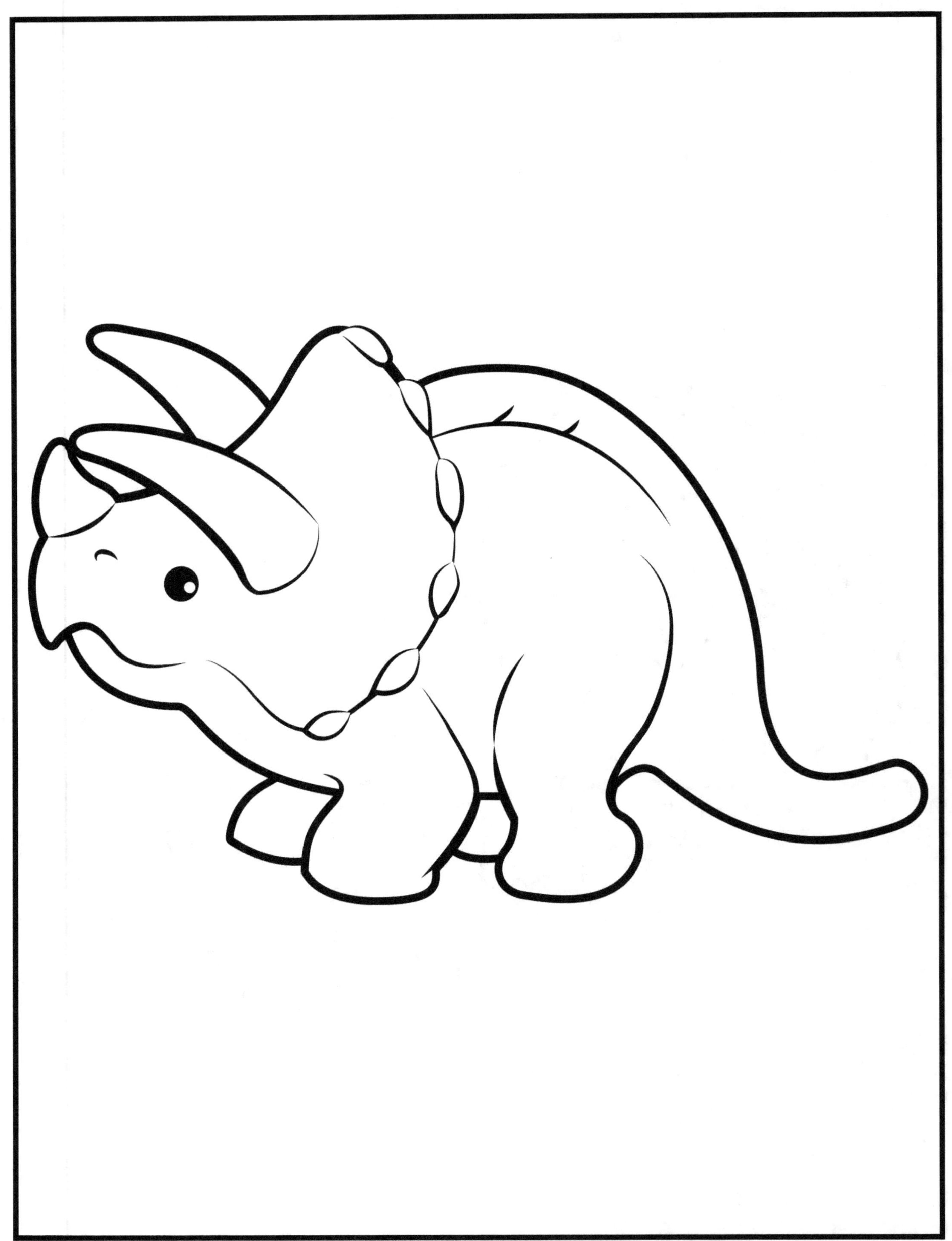

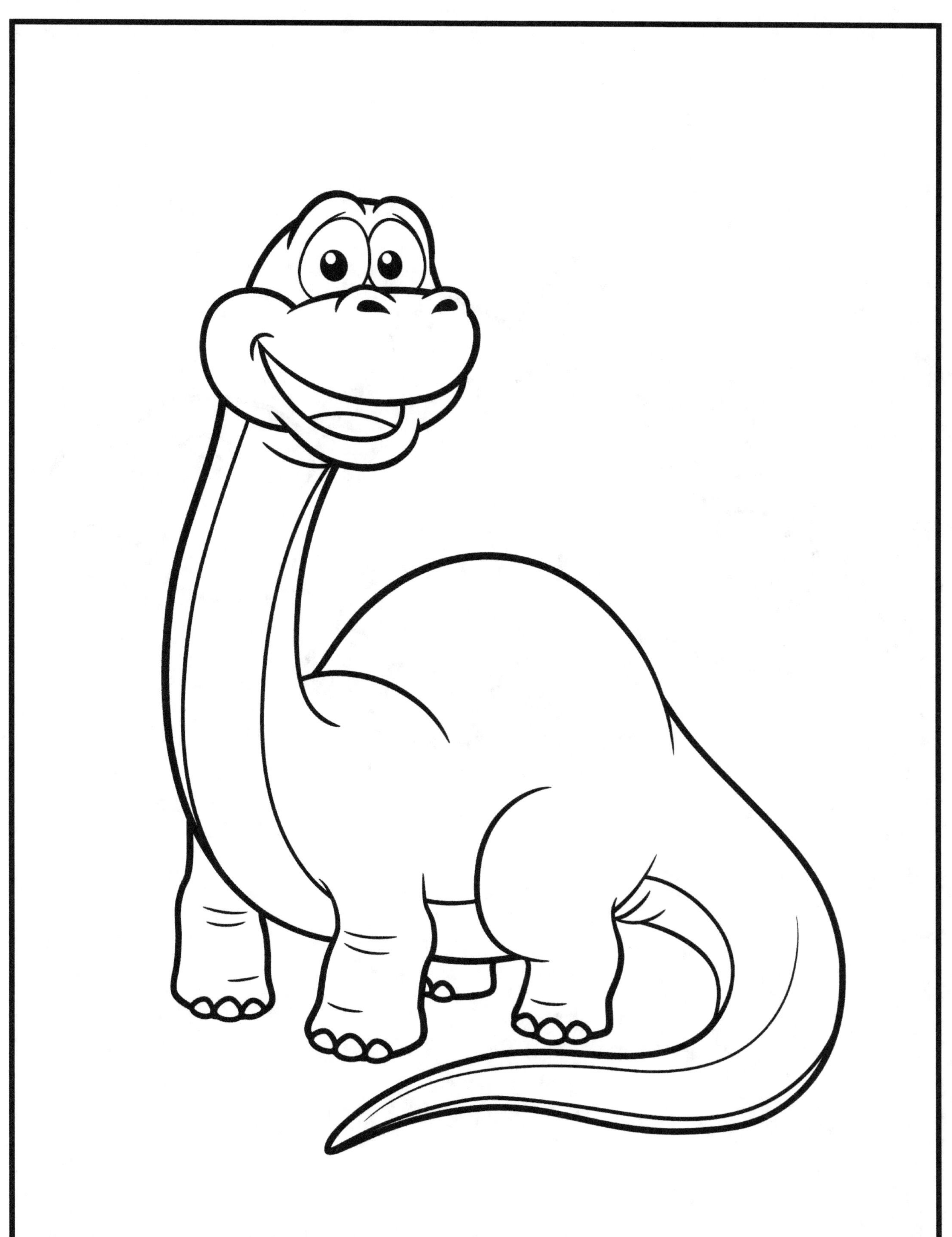

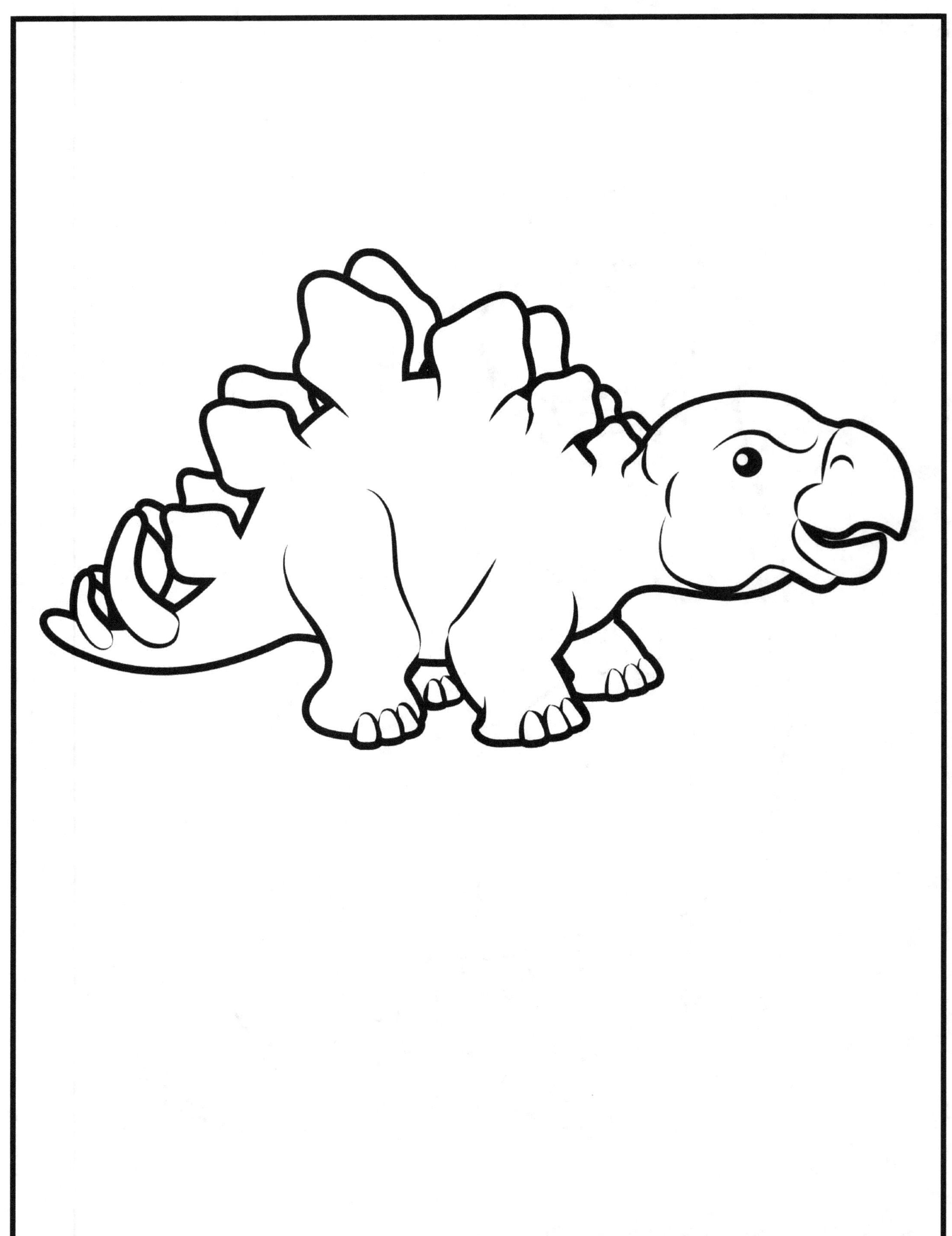

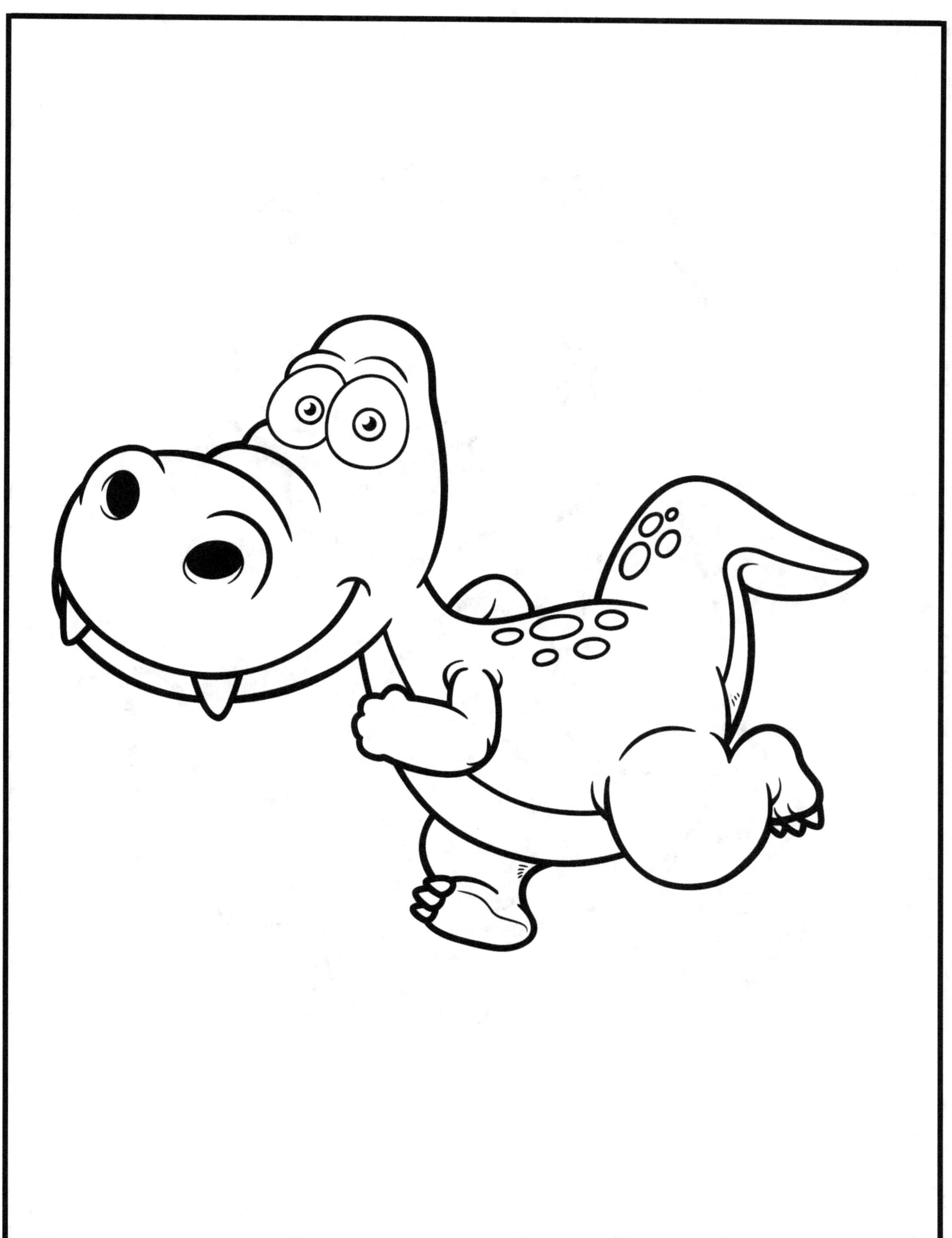

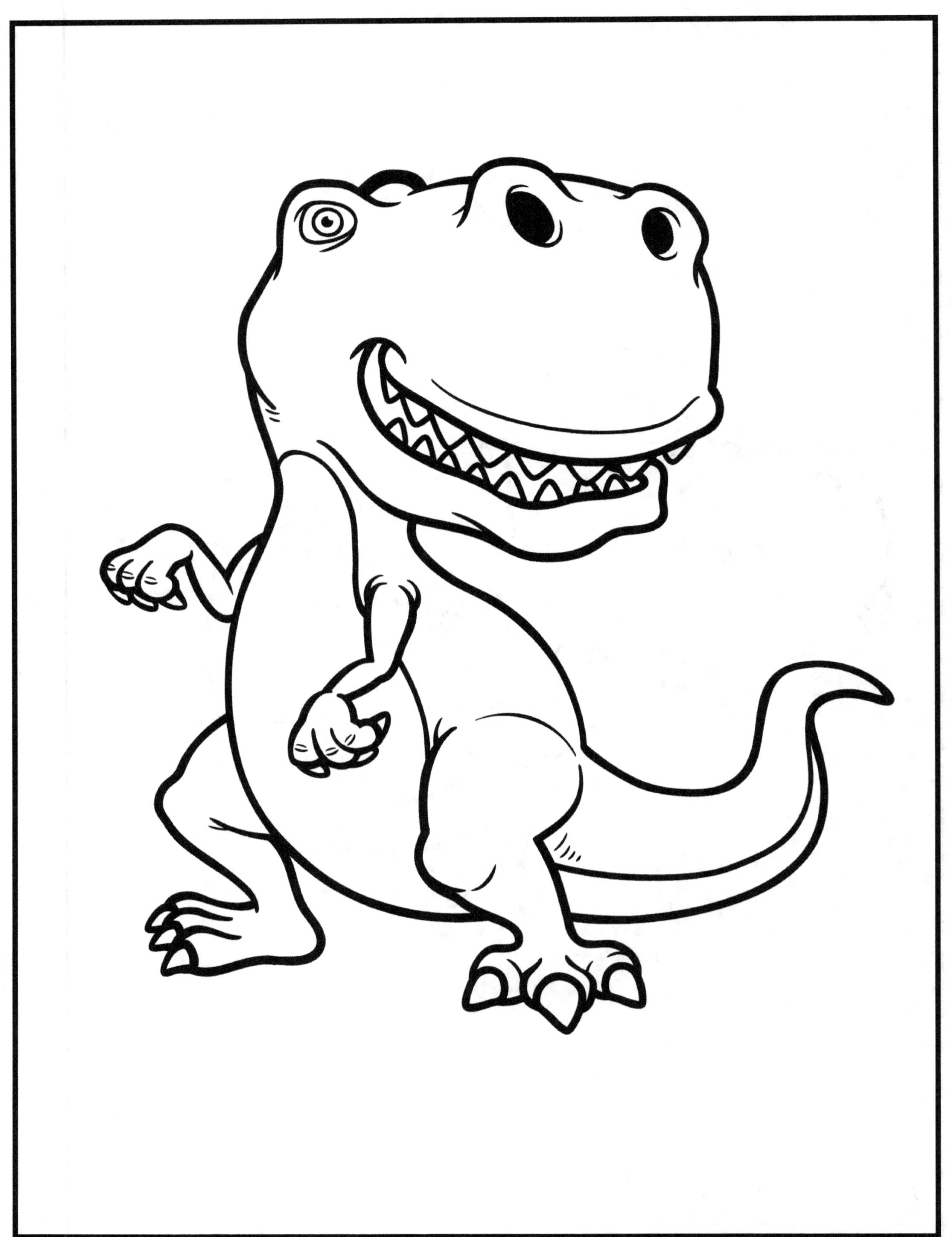

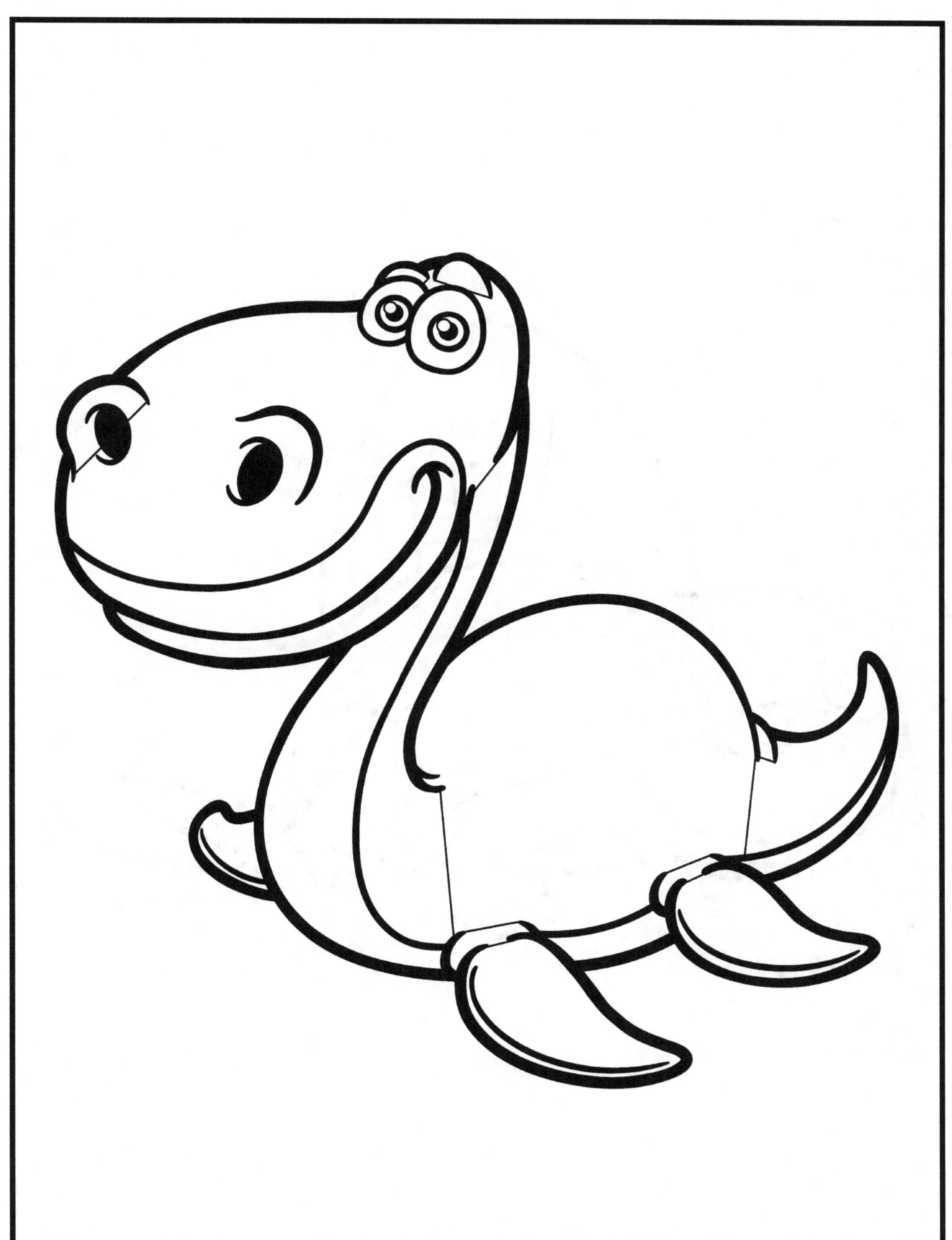

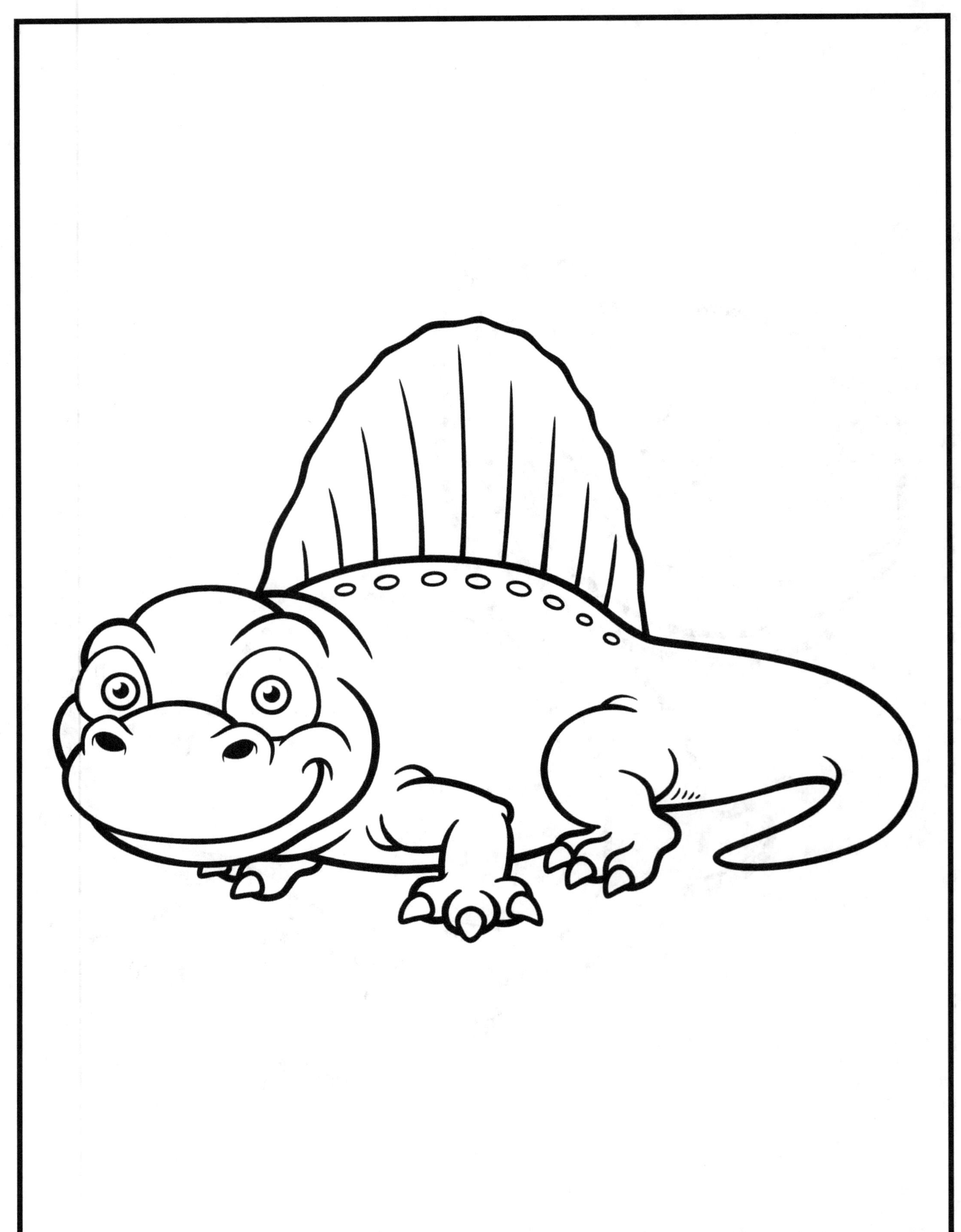

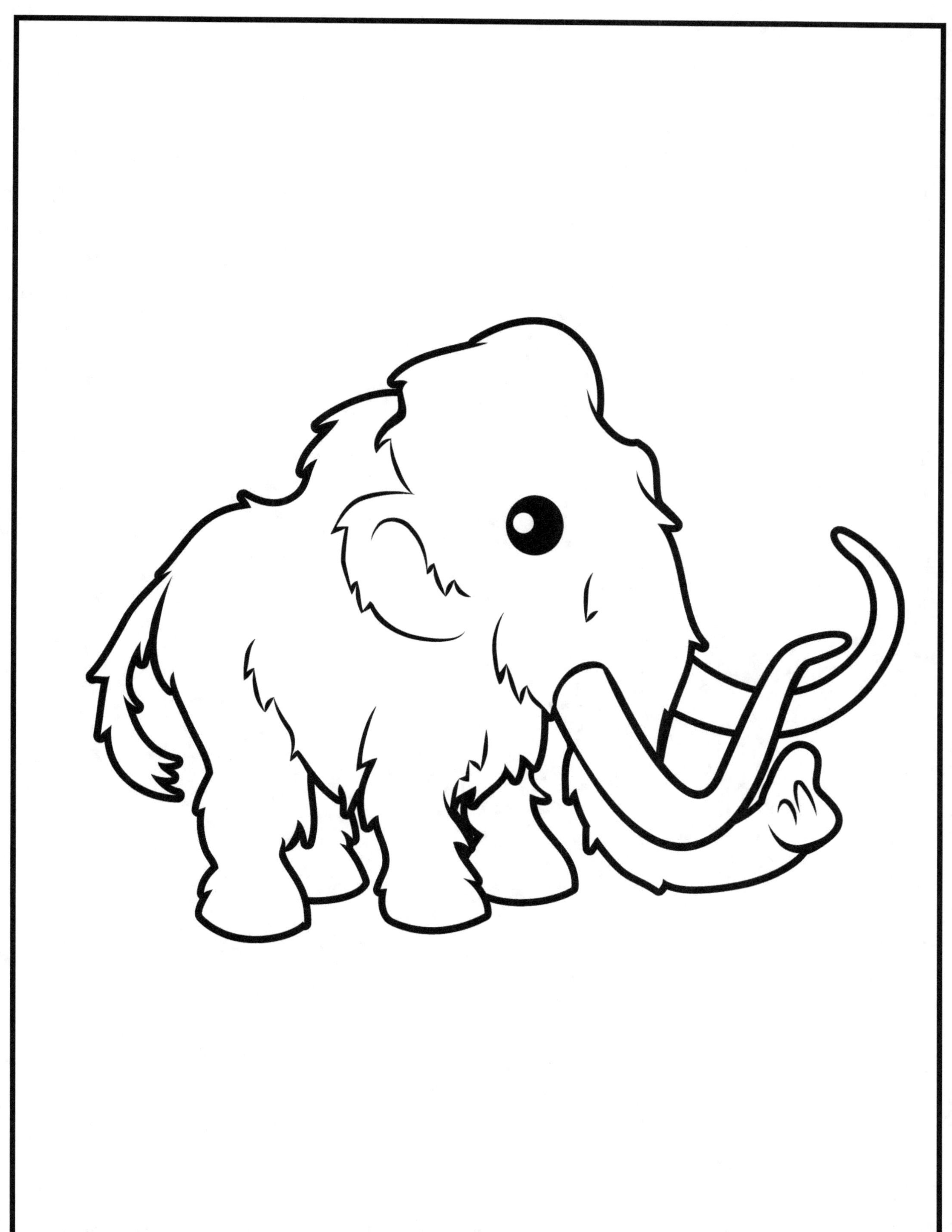

www.ingramcontent.com/pod-product-compliance
Lightning Source LLC
LaVergne TN
LVHW060627170826
845677LV00027B/1694

* 9 7 9 8 8 6 9 4 5 7 3 2 5 *